GOD
IS NOT
NICE

GOD
IS NOT
NICE

Rejecting Pop Culture Theology
and Discovering the God
Worth Living For

ULRICH L. LEHNER
Foreword by **SCOTT HAHN**

AVE MARIA PRESS AVE Notre Dame, Indiana

Nihil Obstat: Reverend Monsignor Michael Heintz, PhD
          Censor librorum
Imprimatur: Most Reverend Kevin C. Rhoades
          Bishop of Fort Wayne–South Bend
November 17, 2016

Foreword © 2017 by Scott Hahn

Founded in 1865, Ave Maria Press is a ministry of the United States Province of Holy Cross. www.avemariapress.com

Paperback: ISBN-13 978-1-59471-748-2

E-book: ISBN-13 978-1-59471-749-9

Cover image © iStockphoto.com.

Cover and text design by Christopher D. Tobin.

Printed and bound in the United States of America

Library of Congress Cataloging-in-Publication Data is available.

To Gerhard Cardinal Müller,
† Fr. Joseph Waas, † Fr. Karl Haller,
and † P. Giovanni Sala, S.J.—
My Teachers in Faith and Theology

CONTENTS

FOREWORD
by Scott Hahn

The fear of the LORD is the beginning of wisdom.
—Proverbs 9:10 (NIV)

This book is long overdue.

Don't worry—I'm not talking about the time you've had it out of the library. I'm talking about the time we Christians have been collectively delusional about God.

It's possible, of course, that this is a constant of the human condition. But I think there's something different about the character of our recent delusions. For at least a century now, we've portrayed God as a nice, sweet, adorable guy—so nice and sweet, in fact, that we couldn't really bring ourselves to adore him.

Eighty years ago, H. Richard Niebuhr lampooned this peculiarly American religion—in which "a God without wrath brought men without sin into a Kingdom without judgment through the ministrations of a Christ without a Cross."[1] And we have succeeded wildly in exporting this therapeutic gospel.

You know it because you've seen it. You can recognize it in the Sunday worship of suburban mega-churches and, I'm sorry to say, not a few Catholic parishes. Find your padded folding chair, and you'll soon encounter a user-friendly God who wants to meet you where you are, affirm and reassure you, and keep you entertained with soothing music for an hour. Incarnate, that God is your "personal Lord and Savior"—*personal*, like a life coach, fitness trainer, or ski instructor.

Ulrich Lehner is not the first to observe that the preaching of this nice gospel corresponds rather exactly to the collapse of Christianity in the global North and West. We may instinctively *like* a nice God—and even go so far as to "like" him on social media. But will we make sacrifices for him and to him? Will we be willing to die for him? Will we make the effort to get out of bed early to praise his name?

Probably not.

Read the Bible from Genesis to Revelation and you won't find the nice, sweet God anywhere. In Genesis he appears with power, he judges with justice, and he promises mercy. His mercy is credible, however, only because his might and justice are manifest.

Read the prophets and ponder the God who appeared to Abraham, Moses, Balaam, Ezekiel, Isaiah, and Daniel—the God whose nearness made them fall down and cover their faces, the God whose light shone upon the hidden corners of their souls.

Nor is this some "Old Testament God" who became obsolete with the New. This is the God Simon Peter encountered in Jesus (Lk 5:8) and John saw in his visions (Rv 1:17).

The God of biblical religion is disconcerting, disquieting, commanding, demanding. He can be shocking.

He inspires awe and something like fear. In fact, Isaiah—whose own call was a frightful thing—lists "fear of the Lord" among the seven gifts of the Holy Spirit (Is 11:1–2).

Such is the God of the scriptures, the creeds, and the sacraments. Consider the words to an ancient eucharistic prayer—words still in our hymnals today.

> Let all mortal flesh keep silence,
> And with fear and trembling stand;
> Ponder nothing earthly minded,
> For with blessing in his hand,
> Christ our God to earth descending
> Comes our homage to demand.

This God comes to us for communion, but he demands the homage that is his right by nature—and our duty by nature. What happens next is astonishing: he gives himself to us as food! Yet it is only astonishing when we know who he is: the Creator, the Almighty, the God who shook the patriarchs and prophets to their sandals.

He has come to be our food, not our antianxiety medication or antidepressant. He has arrived not necessarily to make us feel better but to make us like himself—to make us "partakers of the divine nature" (2 Pt 1:4, KJ21).

The children of God will bear a family resemblance to their Father. "You shall know the truth," Flannery O'Connor said, "and the truth shall make you odd." So we should not be surprised if our neighbors find our faith offensive or even intolerable. The gospel has that effect on people. The poet W. H. Auden told the story of a vicar who "once reduced his congregation to hysterical sobs by a sermon on the Passion." The poor man was dismayed by his success, and he immediately sought to comfort the people in the pews, saying, "Now, please, please don't be upset. Remember this happened a very long time ago. Indeed, perhaps it never happened at all."

The Good News isn't nice, but it's true. The sobbing people knew that far better than their embarrassed pastor.

Ulrich Lehner sees clearly what Niebuhr and O'Connor and Auden saw: that the nice faith is not the Nicene faith. He sees the absurd and self-contradictory nature of this recent project, and he names it. His diagnosis and remedy are more thoroughgoing and useful than any I have seen to date.

The pages of this book are the work of a true theologian. A theologian is one who prays; and one who prays knows that God is changeless but nevertheless wild and not tame. One who prays to such a God knows a God who can be worshiped—knows a God to whom sacrifice can be made—a God for whom we can live and die.

INTRODUCTION
An Image of God
That Isn't True

G od is not nice."

The students in my theology class at Marquette University stirred and shuffled their books. Heads came up. A young woman on my right scrunched her face. A young man on my left frowned. More than a few looked confused. I tried not to smile. It is a moment that every teacher lives for: interaction. Students started to raise their hands, ask questions, and engage with the lecture.

But why? Why did my pronouncement awaken my students from their academic slumber? The answer is very simple: they've probably never heard someone say, "God is not nice." It challenges the dual narrative fed to them by our culture through a twenty-four-hour-a-day bombardment on TV, social media, and, sadly, even at church, telling them that if God exists then God is nice and will do whatever we ask. We can make "deals" with God, or bargain for what we want, as if he is a firm but kindly merchant at a farmer's market.

Or the culture contends that God is some kind of divine thera-pist, and this belief infects even those who attended Catholic schools, as did many of my university students. For them, God is like a psy-chiatrist who treats each of his patients the same way, a friend whom we can call in times of need. But when things are going great, we don't bother him much. Thus, God doesn't play a role in our lives, and grace has no chance to transform us. Why change your life for such a God? He makes no demands.

At first I thought that the religious education these students had received in school and at home contributed to the problem, and it no doubt had. But when I listened to my own kids, as well as the children of others whom I know have been taught since birth about God's character, I realized that they all use the same language. It made me realize just how powerfully the culture shapes the common narrative about God.

If I am to be completely honest, I am not entirely immune to it either. I have often found myself a little too comfortable when it comes to my own relationship with God, making it routine and conventional.

The word *conventional* means ordinary and not very exciting. At best, it is mildly pleasing, forgotten when the next pleasant thing comes along. And in our culture, there are many things to do that delight and surprise. Is it any wonder, then, that students and young adults leave the Church behind? We have made attending church and believing in God something that nice and polite people do, mostly on Sundays. But this is idolatry of the worst kind and a deadly threat to not only our faith but also the faith of our children. Surveys tell us that an overwhelming number of people believe in God or some kind of spirituality. Yet those same people never attend church or ask questions about how knowing God might transform their everyday lives. Instead of seeing God and God's people as a countercultural movement that defies current trends, most people get the impression that God is boring. And so are his people.

This is why we all need the vaccine of knowing the true transforming and mysterious character of God: the God who shows up in burning bushes, speaks through donkeys, drives demons into pigs, throws Saul to the ground, and appears to St. Francis. It is only this God who has the power to challenge us, change us, and make our lives dangerous. He sweeps us into a great adventure that will make us into different people.

At the heart of Marquette University sits St. Joan of Arc Chapel, a fifteenth-century stone structure transplanted from France. Inside is a stone kissed by the saint herself before she went into battle. As a young teenager, Joan met God in a fiery and profound way that changed her life. She came into contact with the wild God and it transformed her into a saint.

Usually I walk by the chapel and pray, "Holy Spirit, help me to guide my students." One day, as I pondered the life of the great saint, I realized I had been conventional about my faith, especially with my students. I had held back my passion for God in the classroom, and I hadn't given my students fuel for their own walk with Christ by inviting them into the mystery of faith. My own faith was drowning in the conventional, the boring, and the unadventurous.

The revelation washed over me, and I felt the burning fire the saints often tell us about: God's love and insight that devours but doesn't destroy. The revelation about the nature of my own faith buckled my knees. I could almost imagine Jesus standing in front of me, as the Challenger, the Listener, and the Healer. I wanted to renew my own efforts to go beyond the safe house I had constructed for Christ and push into trying to find him in all things, as St. Ignatius of Loyola said.

But how to show this to my students? The answer came as I sat in my lush garden and graded their papers. I had asked them to write about the Israelites and their journey out of Egypt—an amazing adventure story of wandering into the desert, drowning armies, and depending solely on God for their daily lives. Yet I often read things such as, "God helped the Israelites because they prayed to him."

This is a true statement. But it doesn't capture the complete picture. I realized that I needed to help my students connect the dots and reject the conventional vending-machine God—that is, the idea that if we put in our coins (or prayers), we will get our goodies dispensed. So in my next class discussion, we talked about the history of redemption in the Old Testament. Abraham was called out of Ur into the unknown. He left everything to follow God merely on the promise that something would be there in an alien land. We talked about Moses and the burning bush, removing his sandals because he stood on holy ground, and about Elijah being fed by ravens and talked to by God in a still, small voice after a great wind and storm. Story after story in the Bible emphasizes the beautiful and strange mystery of God.

And then I said, with more passion than they had probably ever seen from me, "This is a God who invites you on a great adventure that will change your life and who dares you to attempt great things. In the words of Mr. Beaver from The Chronicles of Narnia about Aslan, 'He's not safe, but good.'"

Really, safety in our lives is an illusion. People and events are always changing us, either for good or bad. A great example of this is marriage. When I met my wife at the University of Notre Dame during a class on the Holy Trinity, I knew she would change my life. And she still does on a daily basis. She challenges me to be a better husband and father. It is not a safe situation. I can't rest in my comfort and live in the world of my own head. Rather, the great adventure I began with my wife changed us both.

I told my students that if a *human being* can change us that much and can call us to an amazing journey, imagine what God can do. He takes us on adventures we could never plan and to places we would never expect. God wants us to be transformed, to be uncomfortable in our lives and to stretch toward heaven, a beautiful grace he gives to us.

This grace doesn't make us nice—if it did, it would be just a superficial thing. Instead, it transforms us as wine changes into the Blood of Christ at the Eucharist. It flows from God's very character, and it therefore interrupts all our best-laid plans. We think we know what's best, but God disagrees because he loves us.

St. John of the Cross once wrote, "If you think you can find God in the comfort of your bedroom, you will never find him." The journey to knowing God brings us to places we have not been, helps us notice unseen things, and opens our eyes to surprises and delights we didn't know existed. Only the adventurer is able to see what nobody else sees—and it is this insight that we have lost when we think about God in conventional ways. And then we wonder why life doesn't make sense—why we are so unhappy and why our existence bores us to death. Deep down, we want that challenge, that journey, that adventure.

This book lays out a road map to help us leave the comfort of our bedrooms and meet the wild God who wants our lives. When I first began thinking about this theme, I remembered an episode from my high school days. I sometimes served Mass for an old, retired priest, whom I enjoyed talking with afterward; he had gravitas but also embodied a fierce joy. In one of these conversations, Fr. Karl confided in me that the night before his ordination in 1936 in Hitler's Germany, he knelt in front of the tabernacle and asked God, "Lord, take all that I am, but please don't give me a boring life." His wish was granted. A few years later, he was called to be a military chaplain, serving dying soldiers in Russia. After the war, he almost died in a Soviet gulag, and once he returned to Germany he served in a big parish.

Fr. Karl smiled and said, "And I haven't been bored a single second." He carried no bitterness about the lost years of the war, the pain of prison, starvation, or health problems that deprived him of a career in the Church—just the sincere joy of being a worker in the vineyard of God.

Today, when I stand in front of my theology students, I remember him and his story: with God there is life, a life of adventure. The God whom Catholics believe in is not a nice, conventional being but a radical, all-consuming, at times terrifying mystery.

This book is an invitation to know this God. By discovering who God is, we will find that he invites us to an exciting life but also that he is interested in our eternal well-being. I will try to identify some roadblocks and idols that hinder us from embarking on an adventure with him and suggest how to overcome them. I want to show you how walking with God means adventure in our lives and faith. And, in the end, I hope you realize that God loves you too much to be nice.

THE GOD OF
CREATION

I left my small town for the big city of Munich to study philosophy and theology. Like many college students, I went searching
for my identity, trying to understand how God wanted me to live
my life. Thankfully, many of my professors were Jesuits and knew
how to guide me. One of my philosophy professors suggested I read
Erich Fromm, a Jewish atheist psychoanalyst, and his book *To Have
or to Be?* Fromm's work shook me to the core and woke me up to
my selfishness when it comes to ideas about God.

Fromm believed there are two modes of existence for all human
beings: "having" and "being." Those who focus on "having" want
things and see the world as a backdrop for acquiring and consuming
them. Those who focus on "being" seek to develop the profound
mental and spiritual nature of their inner existence and then strive
to find interconnectedness with the world.

Fromm argued that it is the mode of being that makes us give
up the selfishness of having and helps us become active as true selves,
not as acting machines.[1] I discovered that I was tempted too much
by the conventional mode of life, namely of acquiring and having
things, which explained why I sometimes viewed God primarily as

someone who was there to support my needs. Fromm's book woke me from my selfish slumber and set me on a path to discover the real, personal God of adventure, who was, at times, not very nice.

The Realism of Creation

Fromm encouraged me to discover being; as abstract as it sounds, it was very practical advice, namely, to be mindful of my own existence and my being in the world. This, however, invited me to a deeper understanding of all that is, of all of creation.

The journey to meeting God begins with creation, of which human beings are a part. Even secular environmentalists share with believers the value of nature and the connectedness of humans to it. Yet the Christian faith goes far beyond that. In fact, it is much more radical: we are part of the cosmos and experience our connections within it. We coexist in a hierarchy of being, where the lower is directed to the higher, the material to the spiritual. In the human person, matter achieves a new level because it is connected to a mind and soul. Therefore, we are not permitted to treat the rest of creation badly or abuse it, because we are part of it.

Our body is for us as persons different from what a body is for an animal. Every animal encounters the world as something that satisfies one of its needs: a cat sees the owner who gives food or comfort; a rabbit perceives the plants it wants to eat or a mating partner. As a human being, however, I am able to have a somewhat *fair and unbiased* relationship to this world (absolute objectivity is reserved for God and the angels);[2] I can try to bracket my own desires, expectations, and needs and observe reality for its own sake. I can see the tree for its own sake, not as it serves the beauty of my garden. Or I can reflect on the nature of sexuality rather than see only how it serves my selfish needs. This sort of thinking gives me glimpses into the nature or essence of things themselves and leads me to discover their natural order.

St. Thomas Aquinas taught that the core of true knowledge is "participation," which happens through reception. If we learn to see nature as it is and don't project our expectations and desires on it, we will be surprised and impressed by reality. Nevertheless, very often society hinders us in our ability to see what is going on in the wider world around us.

Many people in our society build conventions that block us from seeing reality. They challenge the notion that things have a "nature." But they forget two points. First, no philosopher ever said that by grasping the nature of a thing we have understood it completely—far from it; so there is no danger that we exaggerate what belongs to the nature of a thing. Second, if we can't grasp *some* essence of a thing, it is very hard to communicate at all. Our words would become meaningless because we couldn't form concepts such as "weather," "animal," or "food." Concepts, however, are only shadows of things, and as Aquinas says, the more we understand something, the more it escapes our conceptual language.[3] The biggest problem is that if we give up the notion of the "nature" of things, we also give up the idea that things have a certain inherent order that we have to respect. It is the forgetting of the natural order of things that enables us to exploit them merely as a resource to be used, whether they are a person, place, or thing.

Very often, we block our view of reality and of the order of things by our bad choices and bad habits: if I am constantly drinking too much, I have attached a wrong value to alcohol, which distorts my view of the world; if I am indulging in pornography, I have a distorted view of human sexuality and the human person; and so on. We have to get rid of the filters that do not allow us to access reality with its hierarchy of goals, its teleology. We have to stop imposing our selfish needs on the world. This is especially the case if we follow the consumer mode of "having," because then we treat others as things, and they become means for our ends.

Human behavior is thus quite different from that of animals, which have a very limited knowledge of things and do not observe the world as world; for them, it is always a world embedded in the context of survival. Humans, however, can choose their stance toward the world. In fact, we are forced to form a relationship with the world because we are not bound by animal instincts. We are forced to be free, and it is in this aspect that we can detect a likeness to God. Thus, we do not see the world entirely as animals do, but we also do not see the world as angels do. Human reason finds order in creation and contemplates the things and beings around us. In this act of becoming watchful stewards of all that is, we are seeing the world a little bit as God does.[4]

Unfortunately, however, we constantly abuse this freedom against divine order. It hit me how much this rebellion against order permeates our life when I was standing in a freezer aisle in the local grocery store, staring at the frozen meat in front of me. How do we treat these animals? Are we seeing them as part of the order, how God wanted them to be treated, how nature "wanted" them to be treated? Our faith has a name for the inclination to disregard God's order, and that is "original sin." In this mode, we tend to see the whole of creation as a means to an end. We utilize the world around us and stop contemplating the order that surrounds and embraces us. Certainly, we do not fail all the time, but we do fail constantly. The philosopher Hans-Eduard Hengstenberg has therefore spoken of *the* major decision in each person's life: we either approach concrete beings according to their inherent order or we surrender them to "our egotistical exploitation."[5] If we decide to see things and persons within the horizon of their natural goals and order, we tend to get to know them more intimately, we learn to love them, and we mature in our will. If, however, we turn away from this order, we see everything only from our own perspective. The first stance is a natural piety toward the entire world, which we can call Christian realism. The second option is what most of the secular world is doing. Of course, we will continue to fail, due to our fallen nature, but the more firmly we decide to approach beings according to their inherent order, the more we will cling to grace and sacramental forgiveness and can hope to make some progress, because we will see the world with "God's eyes" and not through the lenses of selfishness.

Sentimentalism and Its Cure

Realism means being in touch with the real world, with real things. Often I have the impression that we are running away from reality and focusing on feelings as if emotions were the only real thing. Through my experience with religious education textbooks and cat-echesis classes in both Germany and the United States, I have come to see that much of our parish life is centered on sentimentalism, or the chasing of feelings. Children are invited to "feel" and "experience" this or that, but they are rarely given any content for their faith. It does not surprise me that they leave the Church if they can find better feelings elsewhere.

Feelings have their place in faith, but there has to be some substance underneath; otherwise faith has no roots. The churches wanted to be relevant and believed that the only way of achieving that was creating an emotional connection that many thought was lacking in the Church before the 1960s. This experiment has failed in many ways. Sentimentalist theology that preaches religious feeling paved the way for a substanceless religion; Kenda Creasy Dean's book *Almost Christian* proves this painfully.[6] Her statistics show that religious education classes and parental guidance have failed our youth. Three-quarters of religious teenagers today know very little about the *content* of their faith and instead have a benign "whatever" attitude toward religion. They see religion not as connected to the mystery of the world, and thus to realism, but only through their own sense of self: I choose certain beliefs and arrange the beliefs according to my needs or liking. Their God then becomes much like a bad therapist who helps them get over a breakup or offers some emotional help in times of stress. Faith, world, and God are no more than therapeutic means.

It is hard to overlook the egocentrism in this. Do we really need more of this nice, therapeutic God? Can't we acknowledge that the experiment has failed and refocus on the realism of the faith that keeps eroding? When Jesus reminds and admonishes us to become childlike (Mt 18:2–4), he expresses the timeless truth that children are born realists. Only grown-ups will mistake their games with imaginary friends or heroes as misguided reality; every child knows very well what is real and what is not, and if you doubt that, you should spend more time with kids. Imagination is not misguided reality but the ability to see the innumerable possibilities of reality. People who have no imagination have a very limited view of the world and are usually not very creative. While realism is not the same as imagination, imagination without realism is impossible; it is merely delusional.[7]

A child approaches reality as a mystery. She asks why is this rather than that or what makes a chair a chair. She turns a bed into a pirate ship and thus touches upon the mystery of being. The child knows she is part of a great story in which sometimes bedspreads can be ships and chairs can be towers. Little brothers turn into angry pirates. The child knows intuitively that she is connected to a world of beings and meanings. Children contemplate the world—they intuitively approach it with trust. As we grow up, we lose this realism. Our experience is "settled," and we stop gazing in awe at the world; we have become accustomed to it.

As a result, we conceive ideas about the world, trying to make it more manageable because we think childlike wonder is something bad or at least something that distracts us from being productive. Yet as Edith Stein (St. Teresa Benedicta of the Cross) taught us, such "adult" thinking makes us lose empathy! It is therefore adults who are usually less realistic because they have built lenses to filter reality according to their prejudices, preconceptions, and needs. That is why my five children keep me on my toes and are a constant source of inspiration.

Many teenagers and adults think they are no longer a part of the great story of being but stand somewhat outside of it as aloof judges. For them, the world becomes a problem, and *being* is no longer a mystery that contains wonder, excitement, and the road to love. But we cannot separate ourselves from being, since we are always part of it. We can never fully understand what it is; therefore, it will remain in its deepest core an impenetrable mystery. At the bottom of this mystery is, Christians believe, a person, God, who is being itself, or as St. Thomas Aquinas said, the "act of pure existence," on whom all that is depends.[8]

Even in the most fantastic games and imaginary worlds that children create, there is an order and there are rules. In fact, children come up with quite sophisticated, often complicated rules. I remember a board game we never played because we had lost the instructions; yet one day, when I came home from work, I saw four of my kids playing it. They had made up their own rules, and they were quite precise. This is so because children have an innate sense of order. An unclean room where toys lie around is not orderly, some readers might interject—yes, that's true. But when I ask my kids, "Is there order in this chaos? Is it beautiful?" they will grudgingly agree that there is indeed no order and therefore no beauty in the messiness.

Yet for them, the order of things in themselves is more important than the order of the room—they know what is more valuable and joyful and what rules to follow. A child knows intuitively, for example, that an apple tree brings forth apples and that fish eggs produce fish and not frogs. They have an innate understanding of what motherhood and fatherhood are and that life is a gift and not a burden. They know that love is a higher value than money or toys and that death is a great tragedy. As children stumble through the world, they learn how things are connected to each other and that some things are more valuable than others. They develop a natural *hierarchy* of values and of order[9]—until they meet a teacher or parent who tells them that there is no such thing as truth or objective goodness and that their idea of the order of things is merely "relative."[10]

Without Realism, There Are No Convictions

The need for a return to realism is urgent because lack of realism means lack of conviction. If I make the choice of saying yes to realism, I begin trusting the order of things and develop a natural, sympathetic approach to things. Suddenly I realize that reality is not an enemy but rather that I am made to be receptive to the world because it is God's creation. I am made for the adventure of being in this world; this precludes an unhealthy skepticism.

Is this not a bit naïve? some might ask. No, because I am not receptive like a piece of clay. The realism I am arguing for means that I move my mind *intentionally* toward the order of things. I am not pushed or forced without my consent. Being receptive to realism allows for freedom of discovery and freedom of adventure! Without such an attitude toward the mystery of being, without trust and acceptance, I cannot develop a true conviction. And if our churches need one thing, it is convinced Christians! Sincerely held convictions are practically nonexistent in American teenagers: religious beliefs are for them, as Kenda Creasy Dean found out, exchangeable and variable, especially where they could be "offensive" to others. In particular, the conviction of absolute or objective truths is almost universally seen as suspicious or symptomatic of bigotry.

Can the Church survive without belief in truth? If I believe in absolute truth, such as the truth of my faith, it does not follow that I must treat others badly or support religious persecution. In fact, every statement of truth states something absolute, because the nature of truth is that it is absolute. The claim that truths are "relative" is philosophically not coherent, because it is itself a truth claim: the person who says there are no objective truths is nevertheless stating that her sentence is true. You could ask a relativist: "And your belief that truth is relative, do you think that is the right approach to things? Are you convinced of your approach?" "Well, yes." "Well, then, why do you push your truth claim onto me? How can you be convinced of your truth if truth is relative? If it is relative, your truth is relative, and thus you should not be convinced of anything at all because that would mean that there is something better than relative truth claims."[11]

Believing in absolute truth does not mean fundamentalism or intolerance or forfeiting the search for truth—quite the opposite: if I am convinced of a truth, I will not enclose it in a shrine but seek to understand it better, especially if this truth is a person, Jesus, as Christians believe. When I speak about truth claims, I am thinking specifically of these: "Jesus Christ is God and Savior" and "God exists."[12] Both are truth claims, and many Americans would respond, "Yes, I agree, but it's true only for us." Again, such a statement is self-contradicting: either it is true or it is not. Your neighbor can say it's wrong or it's true, but not that it's true for you—that statement simply does not make sense.

We are afraid of denying somebody else's truth claim because we fear being labeled intolerant or bigoted, although it is a sign of *tolerance* that I accept other views that I know are incorrect. Tolerance presupposes a truth claim: I am tolerant of Aunt Lucy's conspiracy beliefs because I love her, but I think she is utterly wrong. Disagreeing with somebody is not the same as hatred or bigotry or intolerance. A relativist, it should have become clear, cannot hold strong convictions and hold them to be true, if she does not want to contradict herself. Yet most do not see this contradiction because they have stopped contemplating the world. If I am a relativist, I will not easily see the intellectual weakness of my stance: I believe in being tolerant, but I do not know that I have given up the idea of truth and thus of tolerance itself.

Truth claims and convictions do not mean that we have to go at one another's throats. Truth does not preclude prudence, justice, fortitude, and temperance—the cardinal virtues are only possible because there is truth, and without truth they are mere chimeras. Without having roots in reality, humans have no truthful convictions but mere *opinions*. But what is a person who is not planted in truth and reality?

Max Picard saw this in his little book *The Flight from God*.[13] We modern men and women, writes Picard, are no longer in real communication with our neighbors, not even with those we love. We uphold external relations, but we run away from the big existential questions, such as, "What is the meaning of life?" that point to God. We tend to exchange the quality of things for mere quantity. Consequently, nothing has value in and of itself. Only through the realism of faith can we regain trust in reality and see it as it actually is. Yet if we keep running away from God, we cannot give up the enslavement to "having things" and to viewing everything from the selfish perspective of its use for us. Only with realism do we have truth, and only with truth do we have conviction and imagination.

Humility, Martyrdom, and Fortitude

Realism teaches humility, which means, literally, "closeness to earth," and thus prepares us to accept the notion of asceticism. The latter entails giving up goods that we are entrusted with, such as food, comfort, and the like, and doing things we do not normally want to do. Pope emeritus Benedict XVI has compared asceticism to physical exercise: we have to do it frequently to prepare our soul for God. We empty ourselves and surrender our will to receive God's. Asceticism plows the soil of the soul so that it can be fertilized by grace: one dies to oneself so that Christ can live in oneself. Christian asceticism, however, is also the utmost realism there is in the world: it perceives that the highest value is God, takes him most seriously, and sees everything in the order it was created or is connected. It aims at keeping mind and will connected to reality and protects us from falling into the trap of viewing God as a vending machine, as the eternal, faceless "principle of the universe," or as a mere set of moral guidelines.[14]

How does all this connect to fortitude, or courage, in my life? Fortitude presupposes, first of all, that I am vulnerable and willing to suffer wounds or death. The Christian concept of fortitude means, in its highest form, martyrdom, the willingness to die for Christ rather than renounce him. However, if I am willing to accept wounds in a fight, I have to know what I am fighting for—I have to know the good. After all, it is for the good that I risk my life. Thus, fortitude needs insight into reality and knowledge of good and evil (that is why Aquinas says that justice and wisdom precede fortitude); one needs strong convictions in order to be brave.

Fortitude does not mean loving risk. It does not mean that I should expose myself indiscriminately to danger but rather that I perceive some things as more valuable than bodily harm. Thus, true fortitude presupposes true realism![15] It is, as Josef Pieper reminds us, not tantamount to being fearless, but it means that fear does not hold us hostage or keep us from facing danger. The two ways of approaching danger are perseverance and attack. For Aquinas, neither is more valuable than the other, but he makes clear that there can be situations in which only holding on to the good can be the last possible way of resistance, a *fortissimo inhaerere bono* ("powerful clinging to the Good").

Anyone who has hung on a rope to climb up a wall or a mountain knows that one has to have a powerful grip and that such action is not at all passive. Holding on to the good in times of peril and resentment, of hatred and slander, is fortitude. St. Teresa of Avila even thought that fortitude was the first and foremost condition for the road to perfection: "I assert that an imperfect human being needs more fortitude to pursue the way of perfection than suddenly to become a martyr."[16]

Without fortitude, I cannot persevere in the long way of a Christian life, and I cannot endure sacrifice and suffering. Only if I am courageous will I be able to act out of conviction, even if it is uncomfortable. Far too often we shy away when things become uneasy. We do not want to offend others—certainly not—yet this does not mean that one has to cede ground to failure and sin. By showing and standing by our convictions gently yet persistently, by having a powerful grip on the rope that connects us with the Holy Spirit, we become witnesses to the one true God, who has called us and the universe into being.

A tame and nice god does not ask for fortitude, because he changes according to the whim of his believers. Such a god also does not prepare us for the final "battle" with death. Yet if I hold on to my faith in fortitude and believe in the wild, adventurous God Jesus talked about, who has called me to a journey with him, I am able to see death not as a catastrophe but as an exchange of life from the worldly to the eternal. Then I can see death as a human action rather than a fate that befalls me. While I will not need fortitude in heaven, I need it to get there—and fluffy religion has nothing to say about it.[17]

This brings me back to my initial comments: if we desire to renew our faith and the Church, we need to make clear what we believe and show that our lives are more connected to the mystery of the universe than to our retirement plan. Convictions are like plants—they need to be nurtured and pruned if they are to grow properly. If they grow wild, that is, if they develop outside the teaching frame of the Church, they can become cancerous.

Let us become like children again in discovering the mystery of reality, strong like the saints in their fortitude and perseverance, and convinced of the truth like Mary, the Mother of God, in the moment of the annunciation, when nothing seemed to make sense.

THE GOD
OF NO USE

A few years ago, I organized luncheons for undergraduate students. Theology professors came, talked about their life stories, and shared why they chose the theological profession. One day, a student asked a good friend of mine, a well-known ethicist, "What is religion good for?"

My friend didn't hesitate for a second as he answered, "Nothing. Religion and theology are absolutely useless." My jaw dropped and the students looked bewildered. After all, the event was designed to recruit the participants to major in theology. For a split second I wondered, even though I knew better, if my friend was going to follow with an atheist rant. Nothing could have been further from the truth, as this well-known theologian explained that the question was all wrong. We don't "use" our faith and religion the same way we use a wrench or a car. The student could hardly be blamed. All of us have asked that question at one time or another. It is the wrong question to ask, but why?[1]

A person who asks "What is religion good for?" isn't really searching for an answer but has already formed an idea of what counts as good or useful. Otherwise, she couldn't ask the question.

Yet that question begs another one: What is the measure for what is good and useful?

Most likely, people measure religion against its contributions to morality, the common welfare, societal progress, the advancement of human rights, and so forth. All these are, of course, important, but if you engage such a question, you concede that religion fulfills a *function*, perhaps even as a by-product. Yet how dare we define religion or faith by its by-products or its latent functions? Would it not be equally questionable to define mathematics by its usefulness for computers?

A latent (that is, unintended) function would be something like the effects of an African tribe performing a ritual dance for rain. The outside observer does not believe the dance will cause rain to fall but rather that it brings the tribe closer together, stabilizes their community. The observer has thus brought to light a latent, unintended function of this dance. Yet if we, as philosopher Robert Spaemann has rightly observed, apply this insight now to the culture of the African tribe, we undermine the role of the rain dance in their society. If you dance to keep the tribe together, all the while knowing that the dancing does not help rain to fall, you will soon stop engaging in this ritual. As a consequence, your society falls apart. It is interesting that we do the exact same thing in the West. We reason about the value of religion for society, drag its societal by-products to light, but do not see that this approach ultimately kills the faith.[2]

Truth Claims Are Not Useful Claims

The biggest conflict arises when we reason about the truth claims of a religion or moral convictions. Sociologists try to explain such truth claims by functions: the religious conviction that giving to the poor is good is explained away as selfish, because it makes us feel good. Also, truth claims we arrive at through reasoning can be "explained" with the help of functions: we claim that stealing is wrong because such a rule stabilizes our society, or we "create" meaning for our lives to escape from lethargy and societal decay. It is easy to see that if we follow this method, all moral and most rational judgments are controlled by something else. Our whole life of meaning, morality, and religion becomes a fiction! The truths of religion, morality, and reason are eliminated. The statement "I believe in Jesus Christ" is only a function—it consoles me, helps me to deal with my life, but it isn't *true*! We could no longer say that the simple principle that it is our duty to do good and to avoid evil is true.

Nobody has seen this clearer than Friedrich Nietzsche, one of the fathers of modern atheism. He saw that explaining morality and religion through their functionality only undermines them, or simpler, "by relativizing the absolute, the absolute is eliminated."[3] Keiji Nishitani, a twentieth-century Japanese philosopher, reminds us that the way to refute Nietzsche and the functionalizing of religion is not to engage in the game at all. We have to answer the question, Why religion? with the counter-question, Why do we exist?

> We become aware of religion as a need, as a must for life, only at the level of life at which everything else loses its necessity and its utility. Why do we exist at all? Is not our very existence and human life ultimately meaningless? Or, if there is a meaning or significance to it all, where do we find it? When we come to doubt the meaning of our existence in this way, when we have become a question to ourselves, the religious quest awakens within us. These questions and the quest they give rise to show up when the mode of looking at and thinking about everything in terms of how it relates to us is broken through, where the mode of living that puts us at the center of everything is overturned. This is why the question of religion in the form, "Why do we need religion?" obscures the way to its own answer from the very start. It blocks our becoming a question to ourselves.[4]

According to Nishitani, questioning the usefulness of religion hinders us from getting to the heart of God. It puts a veil over the profound question of our existence and the meaning of our life. Only if we put aside all ideas about utility can we really assess the existential questions of life. Those questions lead us to religion, which offers an answer to our quest for meaning.

Belief Changes Our Perspective

You see, belief in God is not something "useful." It is a change of perspective. Belief provides a new horizon. A person who believes in Jesus Christ holds that the world was created by an all-loving God and that this God has loved and wanted them since before their existence. Without God, our existence ends at our death, and all our achievements will be gone. Ultimately, then, our life is meaningless and makes no difference if there is no God. After all, humans are just a by-product of evolution and there is no objective good or evil; the rabbit outside in my garden, in this view of the world, is as valuable as I am. However, *if* God exists, then the perspective changes, especially if the Christian story is true. If true, God offered humanity a special place and special access to him and gave humans an immeasurable dignity.

Thus, because religion changes our perspective and outlook on life, questions about the usefulness of religion do not make sense, just as nobody would ask about the usefulness of kind treatment in a romantic relationship.

If you are familiar with the New Testament, you probably know that the first letter of John identifies God with love (1 Jn 4:8), but you may not have thought about what this really means. Love always intends and aims at a higher value. The lover perceives something in the beloved that corresponds to such a higher value. This value, however, has to be connected to the absolute, because otherwise it would be impossible to judge higher and lower examples of such a value. We can say that Jesus' love is unconditional because we can compare it with the love or absence of love we encounter among humans. If the value we experience in the other is not intimately connected to an absolute value, we would have to judge our love as merely subjective. Then, however, the beloved would not be truly and objectively worthy of our attention and love. Would we irrationally decide to love her anyway? That would not only destroy the beauty of relationships but also make reasonable and dignified human behavior impossible. Only because the lover relies on the idea of the absolutely valuable as a person—that is, God—can he perceive the beloved as participating in this value. In the Middle Ages, one called this the argument from the gradation of things. If there is no highest value, we have no way to measure what is lower or higher, and if that is true, then true interpersonal love as the perception of a higher value is impossible.[5]

Yet it is not only love that changes our view of life; it is also death. I remember vividly a graduate class with the late John S. Dunne at the University of Notre Dame, who, with his unforgettable smile and sparkly blue eyes, told us twenty-four-year-olds, "When I turned twenty-seven, I realized my youth was over and that death awaited me." My mother had just died the year before, followed soon by my grandfather and my favorite uncles, so Professor Dunne's words went straight to my heart. I was mortal, too. That was the kind of existential experience this wise teacher was able to bring about in class.

Some critics of religion believe that religion is just a coping mechanism for the fear of death. But from Professor Dunne and others I have learned the exact opposite is true.[6] In fact, the criticism that religion is just a function helping us deal with our mortality, and that consequently all of its truth claims are fairy tales, is based on two false premises. The first is that religion deals mainly with the elimination of our fear of death. The second is that religion is a coping mechanism that cannot be true—which is a logical fallacy (genetic fallacy), since the origin of a truth does not determine whether it is true or not; a notorious liar can give us a true statement, even a delirious person. But since so much ink has already been spilled over the second premise, let's return to the first. If it were true, the globe would be filled with religious people. Religion would be universal. How could we explain, then, the rising number of those who do not "need" religion? If we look closer at the increasing number of nonreligious people and ask in what they believe, we almost always get the answer, "I believe in science."

Science is, in my view, the number one coping mechanism of humans to deal with the inescapable truth that we and everything we produce will some day cease to exist (at least on this planet). That is the reason we pay doctors more than philosophers: they keep death and pain away from us. Although we do not realize it, entertainment is the second-biggest contingency coping mechanism: we pay sports heroes, movie stars, and entertainers so much because they distract us from the ultimate conclusion that we are mortal and that our life is meaningless without God.[7] In reality, religion does not so much solve the problem of mortality as *create* it. Now this needs a bit more clarification.

Perhaps religion helps some to deal with their short life span by assuring them of an eternal life to follow, but why does the question, *Why is the world as it is?* even arise? If we looked at the world as a rabbit does, we would see it as a series of functions that help us to survive. The world seen as a complex thing that has come into existence, could be different, and will go away, presupposes that we understand some bigger meaning that transcends this world. By asking the question, Why is the world as it is? we recognize that nothing in this world is absolutely necessary; everything is contingent. We ask this question not as scientists but as regular human beings—and when we do, we appeal to a higher idea that lies beyond the brute fact of the world's existence. If the universe is simply there, that is no answer to the "why." Bertrand Russell, one of the great atheist philosophers of the last century, aptly summarized that the world "just is"—it is a brute fact about which we cannot reason because that would undermine atheism and smuggle in the religious question. Thus, religion brings up the question of why things such as pain, death, and mortality exist. Religious faith makes us uncomfortable in the universe by pointing beyond it without giving us a hands-on answer. Therefore, the argument that religion is supposed to be a coping mechanism for mortality doesn't convince me.

Where Culture and Faith Clash

But how then can an outsider understand religion and religious practice if questions about functions are wrongheaded? When we are asked by non-Christians, should we not try to articulate why our religion is useful to others? Yes and no.

I think it is impossible to get a real understanding of religion without any religious commitment. One will not understand the essence even if one has discovered all kinds of "functions" and is able to describe religious phenomena. An ethicist has to be ethical and can't stand outside ethics. Likewise, a person who wants to fully understand religion has to stand within a religion. Philosophy can help us articulate questions about the religious dimensions of our lives, which can be helpful for those searching, but we should avoid engaging the game of usefulness or relevance at all costs.

It is disheartening to see this game played, especially in contemporary politics. Politicians who are afraid of confessing their religious convictions try to describe religious beliefs as "cultural values." This, of course, means that religions are good because they contribute some values to our culture. But what are these values, and are religious values and cultural values identical? For Max Scheler, the philosopher who shaped the mind of St. John Paul II, religious values are at the heart of our value experience. Moreover, religious values are values of the Holy. The values of the Holy are not just intensive forms of other values, such as beauty, goodness, and truth, but they are also independent. One can best apprehend this thought if we try to visualize what we mean by a holy person: a holy person is not just an improved version of a genius, a sage, a just person, or a lawgiver. "Even a human being who would be all that, would not cause the impression of being holy."[8] With precision and persuasion, Scheler demonstrates that the Holy is of a totally different value sphere, one that we encounter in the depth of our souls. If we *confound* it with values of our culture, we exterminate the aspect of the Holy in religion, the experience of God and his reality. Or to put it in plainer words, we drag God's values down into the mud of our world.

Equally disastrous is the idea that religion is needed as an additional value, as if it were a necessary vitamin supplement for society. If religion is a supplement, then culture must be the whole that really counts. Yet culture is something finite, created by humans, like art or education. Thus it makes no sense that religion can supplement culture. We can't sprinkle God on society like magical glitter. It is the other way around: culture has to open itself up to God, searching for the true, good, and beautiful; by doing so, it can be shaped by the divine.

Either religious values are the highest—because they are experienced in God, the source of all goodness, beauty, and truth—or they are superfluous projections of our subconscious.[9] If we insist on the independent sphere of religion and of the values of the Holy, not by invoking Bible verses but by invoking reason, we can save our belief from being abused. Then society will take us more seriously, because we are not claiming to be the icing on the cake but rather people with a message that will transform the world.

Scheler urged his generation to "liberate" religion from being abused as a stabilizing force for society. Belief in God does not exist to keep crime rates down or support mental health. In contemporary society, this attitude can be seen in the countless social organizations religions sponsor; of course, these are worthwhile endeavors that help those who are marginalized and exploited. However, they also tend to make the core of religion—the personal encounter with the Holy—disappear. Only if the Holy is at the heart of religion, and truthful social justice that is more than activism flows from it, will our children understand that they do not need "values" to be "better people." They need to be transformed.[10]

In my ten years teaching at a Jesuit university, I have seen my fair share of soulless activism pretending to be Christian, Catholic, or Jesuit. Once such habits take root, they are very hard to change, and they suffocate every attempt at contemplation because the Holy is perceived as a threat to the emptiness of the activists' own agenda. I have witnessed students working insistently for scheduled hours of eucharistic adoration and struggling to raise money to buy a monstrance while money was freely spent on conferences pertaining to dialogue, diversity, and social justice.

The Welcome Trap

Taking our religion seriously does not mean that we marginalize others or make them feel unwelcome. Yet that is what many theologians and pastors believe. As a consequence, they have stopped being missionaries. The consequence of this misunderstanding is a mistaken religious pluralism: all religions are equally good and equally wrong; their value stems from what they contribute to society. Then Christians begin to believe that only relativists are good citizens.

Are people with religious truth claims and beliefs necessarily marginalizing others? Does it logically follow that somebody who believes passionately in Christ as his savior would be unwelcoming to an atheist or create a hostile atmosphere? Certainly, there are many cases in history that seem to prove this, and the usual suspects are religious fanatics overseeing persecution of dissenters or preaching condescending values. But if we look closer, the picture changes. Then we see that most cases Church critics cite are examples of what Scheler has called "enslaved religion," a religion entangled in politics and the game of usefulness. For example, the French Catholics of the seventeenth century were certainly hostile to the Huguenots, but it was because religion and secular politics were so closely intertwined. It is mostly secular ideologies that are marginalizing others, usually motivated by the desire to increase power, influence, and revenue. Passionate believers are not necessarily intolerant fanatics. The fact that we discuss values and ideas is part of the very nature of a free society. That we do this in respect for each other is a given, yet respect for the other does not mean one has to agree with the other's lifestyle choices or views on the world.[11]

Secular ideology claims to be tolerant but is in itself a sort of evangelizing cult. Secular and religious pluralists preach that no one should try to convince others to give up their faith and seek to convert others, because there is no objective truth.[12] Yet they preach just that, an objective truth (namely, that there is no truth!). They believe it with passion; it is unfortunate that they do not realize this logical contradiction.

My point is that belief in God is either a truth claim or it is not. A god whom we "like" because he gives me and my neighbor some morals that make it less likely that we will become the victims of theft or murder is not God but a function. Unless we have the strong conviction that God exists, and do not shy away from stating such as truth—rejecting the popular thinking of "that may be true for you but not for me" as shallow and self-defeating reasoning—our faith is lost. When this view is prevalent, our society becomes, in the words of Pope Benedict XVI, a "dictatorship of relativism." The silence of dead convictions will no longer cry out, as witnessed in our churches, which have become very, very quiet places already. One cannot imagine that the White Rose, a resistance group in Nazi Germany, or Dietrich Bonhoeffer, who also resisted Hitler to the point of sacrificing his life, would have done so for a god who simply fulfilled some function in society. If push comes to shove, "only people with convictions resist,"[13] and at the present moment we risk our future by withholding this truth from our children.

THE GOD OF OUR IMAGINATION

Whenever I teach an introductory course in theology, I ask my students, "If you died tonight, why should God let you enter heaven?" The most frequent answers I hear are variations of "I have done good things, and I haven't killed anybody or committed adultery or theft. I am a good person." Many of these students have gone through twelve years of Catholic education.

You can imagine the reaction when I tell them what the Church really teaches. That is, no one actually deserves heaven. The shocked outrage pulses throughout the room.

To diffuse the anger, I take them through a thought experiment. I tell them, "Let's say you live eighty years. Of these eighty years, you are able to use reason and be morally responsible perhaps for seventy of them. Within this time span you get married, have a couple of kids, grandkids, you help some people, give a bit to charity, and retire happily. For the relatively few good actions in a finite life, you should earn an infinity of bliss and happiness? That sounds like a Ponzi scheme!"

I am not saying they are fully convinced by this argument. But it makes them examine themselves in a more honest fashion and realize that nothing we do by ourselves makes us worthy of heaven. Only Christ's grace does—and it is his life in us and only that which gives our actions merit.

The Temptation of "Good Works"

The Church rejected my students' views in the fourth century by declaring Pelagianism a heresy. Pelagius was a pious monk who lived in the fourth century and believed in free will but also stressed that it is our good works that save us. For St. Augustine, Pelagius's view did not make sense. If we can merit salvation, then Christ died in vain, Augustine reasoned. Consequently, the Church clarified publicly that nobody can work herself into heaven. If we are saved, it is only by the grace of Jesus Christ, and our works are only meritorious because of Christ's merits. Only if we "bet" on Christ and his grace, as the philosopher Pascal said, will we win eternal life.

Why do so many of our contemporaries have a problem with this basic, universal Christian doctrine? Why is it that almost all Catholics are secretly (whether they realize it or not) Pelagian? I think one of the main reasons lies in the development of modern thinking in the last three hundred years and the current culture of individualism.

Before the nineteenth century, gifts among commoners were something special. One had little time and little money to spend on unnecessary things; nevertheless, one could still appreciate a gift, knowing that one could probably not reciprocate the favor. Real gifts are always undeserved—such as the gift of life. In Genesis chapter eleven, we find the story about the infamous tower of Babel, but what seems to be the central theme of this myth is not the tower itself, which God did not destroy, but the hearts of the humans who built it. They are portrayed as self-centered; they achieve things just for themselves—they do not appreciate their talents and lives as gifts from God. Therefore, God punishes their pride and confuses their language but does not destroy their beautiful city. The Genesis story encapsulates not only what the Israelites saw in the Babylonian exile but also what Christians experienced in the Industrial Revolution in the eighteenth century: a new "city culture" developed in which humans worked only for themselves and forgot the most basic human moral attitude of gratitude. By thinking everything was in their reach, the ancient people of Babel—as well as our modern forefathers—eliminated God and also the idea that everything they achieved was done with gifts from above.

By throwing out gratitude, we also got rid of humility. And the departure of these virtues has changed our image of God. If we are no longer fundamentally grateful and humble, God is no longer in the picture because "we can do it our own way." I am not saying that we should not be proud of our achievements, but rather that we realize where they originate. If we fall into the trap of believing that we are "lords of our lives," we will also go down the road of deceiving ourselves that we can make it to heaven without God.

The Disappearance of Divine Providence

Up until the time of the Enlightenment, most people knew what divine providence was, and most believed in it. It was not understood only as God's foreknowledge of the future but also and especially as his way of directing and guiding the world. In other words, people knew that God was active in the world. Some theologians invoked providence to explain the beauty of creation. They wrote detailed essays, for instance, about the perfect adaptation of spiders to their environment, the intricacies of plants, and the complex nature of human anatomy. Although such arguments for intelligent design are problematic theologically and scientifically, they bear witness to the strong conviction that all that exists is governed by the wisdom of God.

In 1755, an enormous earthquake shook Lisbon, Portugal, and destroyed large parts of the predominantly Catholic city. With thousands dead, many asked how providence could have permitted such a catastrophe. The questions people raised went beyond justifying God's permission to allow such things to happen. Rather, most seemed shaken because of their overall conviction that the world and the course of history were directed by a wise lawgiver.

Many Enlightenment philosophers came then to the conclusion that we are on our own. Most famously, the German Immanuel Kant argued that one could never objectively say that this or that event was caused by divine providence. Ultimately, he thought, with Voltaire, the hero of the French Revolution, that we have to be the masters of our own fortune—otherwise, we will remain inactive and lethargic.

Of course, they were right in one respect: we cannot prove that something is directly caused by divine providence. Yet, with Aquinas, we can say that God not only keeps the world in existence but also has endowed the world with the power of causality so that it may bring forth "things" and events. So if a weather change caused locusts to descend on Egypt at the moment that Moses predicted God's judgment, this weather change was a secondary cause. It brought about what God wanted through the laws of nature, which date back to God as the primary cause of all that is.

The Puppet-Master God

Nevertheless, Kant went further. He believed that any external guidance of our mind would destroy human freedom. That is, grace that helps and transforms us would be like a leash that also restrains us. For Kant, we have to be fully competent to reach our goals and aspirations without divine help. To trust in divine providence, as supposedly Christians did, was for him immoral: if one expected to be guided by providence and grace, one did not have to develop moral virtues and follow the norms of morality but was moved like a dummy by the puppet master!

It is surprising how an intelligent man such as Kant believed in such a caricature of Christian faith. He could not comprehend that grace and freedom complement each other. Human freedom and divine providence are in no way enemies or rivals but rather work together. Aquinas remarked most famously that grace never destroys nature but perfects it. This principle is also at work in our actions.

Grace and freedom cooperate so that human freedom is fully responsible. Therefore, grace does not limit my options but liberates me to be really free. Alcoholism offers an excellent example. If you suffer from this addiction, you are constantly tempted by the presence of a liquor bottle; that temptation will *never* go away. Grace would be like the AA meetings that give an alcoholic the strength to counter his addiction. The sponsor and the meetings do not destroy the freedom of the person trying to deal with his addiction; they help him recuperate from it. These causes cooperate with him and open up a world of possibilities that was closed to him beforehand. How could grace then make us unfree?

Certainly, one can fall back into old ways if one is not constantly aware that without a support network, one is not able to withstand addiction (or sin). It is the same with grace: we cannot persevere without it. Yet this realization runs against everything we have been taught in our culture since the Enlightenment. We are told to be independent and free, not to need anything or anybody. Ironically, however, we are told what to think by advertising agencies or so-called authorities informing us what we need or want. The fact that we rely on what these people tell us shows how much we need someone or something to save us from the gigantic hole in our hearts that is sucking us into the void.

Thus, when Pope Francis mentioned that he views the Church as a hospital for the sick and sin junkies, everyone considered this a new idea. Many view the Church as an institution that smooths over their life's problems and edges, like a genie who fulfills our wishes. Grace, however, can only work if we accept it and let it flourish, and for that to happen, we have to confess to being "addicts" who need help.

Not only do we want to be independent but we also do not want "gifts" because we feel that we deserve things. Grace does not work that way. Although the Church has always taught that God gives every person sufficient grace to come to the faith, nobody is *entitled* to receive God's gifts. We are creatures—he is God. He has no obligation toward us. Besides, as we saw before, a heavenly reward of eternity is disproportional to the few good things we can accomplish in a lifetime.

The Fine Print of Grace

Grace as the self-communication of God is something very personal. It requires openness of the human heart. In Pope Benedict XVI's words, it requires the insight that there was somebody who loved me long before I did anything that was lovable.[1] Such love is a gift.

In the mentality of our times, gifts have become a burden: if my children receive a twenty-dollar present at a birthday party, I feel obliged to give a present of similar value back at the next party. These are no longer real gifts but exchanges of niceties.

Yet we are reminded every year of the true nature of gifts on Christmas, when parents give their children presents without expecting anything in return. Despite all the usual complaints of excessive consumerism, the holiday seems to have preserved at least this important message. Outside this season, however, we usually feel awkward if presents are given to us without the expectation of something in return. We assume a hidden agenda behind such an act of kindness, a trick—everybody wants something . . . For most, it would require an almost superhuman act of overcoming self to accept such a gift as merely a gift.

Some modern sociologists would say that the exchange of presents is a necessary ritual humans have invented in order to show favor and sympathy. That is, such rituals were adopted to ease tension and make communities stable. Perhaps, but that creates a problem for our view of God. If we adhere to these ideas, then we might expect an agenda behind God's offer of eternal life—you have to *do* something to get to heaven. Yet heaven is closed for humans—period.

Yes, there are no humans in heaven. How can I say that? Is that not heresy? No. What I mean is that it is absolutely unimportant *what* we do. As ourselves, we do not enter heaven. We have to *become somebody else* by being transformed through Jesus Christ. Only as transformed children of God do we enter the kingdom. By offering to move into our souls and hearts, God promises to change us and enable us to do works that are full of merit. Without his grace, however, these works, as morally good as they may be, are worthless.

If you are in a state of grace, you are following Christ, and your works reflect what Christ wants you to do, because he lives in you. It is the grace of Christ, not your doing, that makes these works "meritorious." These actions are your gifts of love that participate in Christ's love and therefore are rewarded with God's gifts (*CCC*, 2006–2011), the most beautiful of which is eternal life with him.

The philosopher Dietrich von Hildebrand has summarized this ancient Christian teaching in his magnificent book *Transformation in Christ*. This transformation requires radical change: "A strong desire must fill us to become different beings, to mortify our old selves and re-arise as new men and women in Christ. This desire, this readiness to decrease so that 'he may grow in us,' is the first elementary precondition for the transformation in Christ. . . . Our surrender to Christ implies a readiness to fully transform us, without setting any limit to the modification of our nature under his influence."[2]

Hildebrand nails it. A person first has to surrender in order to be transformed by grace. Surrender is no armistice but unconditional capitulation. This requires a willingness to lay down my life and goals and plans. In other words, I have to be willing to accept that I suddenly have a Lord over me. It is painful to sacrifice my personal freedom, but it is the only way that freedom can be elevated and transformed.

Because it is painful, surrender looks unattractive. Therefore, many wonder if it is really necessary to surrender. Could I not make a compromise with God? Could I not accept him as Lord but keep his disturbing influence away from my lifestyle? In the image of the poet George MacDonald, I feel threatened that the architect will rebuild my comfortable house and turn it into a palace, going beyond the limits of any reasonable budget. I feel terrified because I realize he wants to move in with me. If I do not accept the gift, I do not undergo transformation; but if I do a little for God, I should at least get some reward—it doesn't have to be a palace! I think, then, that living a "good life" and "doing good deeds" can earn me a spot in God's realm without giving up my old self—without dying to myself. The Church, however, has always rejected such bargaining with God.

Moralism Won't Save Us

At the core of such a view are Pelagius's two main doctrines: that Christ died only for those who choose to sin, and that some can be saved by virtuous works. Pelagius was not "godless," as Karl Barth branded him, but rather a Christian moralist who tried to answer the question of what constitutes the value of human actions. St. Augustine, however, made clear that this view has devastating consequences: if I can earn my spot in heaven, then the death of Christ was not the unique event that opened heaven's gates. It was ultimately unnecessary. But for Augustine, and for us, such a view is contrary to the faith. After all, at the center of our faith is the celebration of Jesus in the Eucharist as the new *sacrificial* lamb. I believe that most modern Pelagians are not aware of these consequences of their thought. Otherwise, they would realize how utterly un-Christian their stance really is.

Why is it so tempting to think that one can obtain heaven through good works? I do not believe that we should blame medieval Catholicism as so many hastily do. Enlightenment philosophy seems to be the more plausible culprit. Yet there is another explanation. In the nineteenth-century process of industrialization, when free market capitalism steamrolled the Western world, the number of those dependent on factory jobs increased dramatically. While in earlier generations one could be to some degree self-sufficient, this was no longer possible in an industrialized city. Wages and salary increases became much more important, and in consequence, this mind-set was also applied to moral actions: What do I have to do to get proper compensation in the afterlife?

Heaven became just like any other business deal: an exchange of goods. After all, God was, as the father of economics, Adam Smith, declared, interested in our happiness, and God's goodness depended on how he distributed his favors. God was no longer glorified for who he was. Instead, he was worshiped only insofar as he guaranteed human happiness, as long as he "did" something for us. He became a "thing," which was only good to get something else. God ceased to be the highest good in itself, as classical theology had taught. That's why there is a chasm between Aquinas and Adam Smith!

For Aquinas, God also guarantees our happiness, but for him happiness is *in* God and not a separate thing. For Smith, happiness is not communion with God but a state of pleasantness produced by him. Perhaps this analogy will help us understand Smith's position: we are invited to a dinner to honor a great person, but we only attend the event because of the food that is served there. I think this understanding of Smith becomes obvious when we read his book *The Theory of Moral Sentiments*, where he acknowledges, "The divine being contrived and conducted the immense machine of the universe so as at all times to produce the greatest quantity of happiness."[3]

For Smith, God works this quantitative happiness by creating us in a way that makes us *unable* to have sympathy with one another in our sufferings and sorrows; we are rather programmed by God to connect to others by emulating their wealth and prosperity. Yet if we are to imitate each other's search for wealth because it is according to the divine plan, then it is works that save us. Smith acknowledges this when he says that indeed through active "beneficence" of our good actions we find "mercy" in the eyes of God and thus forgiveness.[4] Such beneficence, however, is only possible if we are at ease with ourselves, free and without coercion. Therefore, Smith abolishes the need for grace, because if traditional Christianity were true, then the necessity of grace would render the "sentiment of imitating each other's search for prosperity" worthless.

Aquinas's view of God could not be more different. For him it is clear that honor, power, and wealth—all the things Smith thinks are important—can *never* make us happy because they are not ultimate ends and that we need grace to be freed from our own selfishness.

Nevertheless, the temptation to follow Pelagius or Adam Smith persists. It is so much easier to treat eternal life as the cash distribution at the end of a life insurance policy whose good work premiums we have regularly paid. What strikes me, however, is that the Smith theology talks about an abstract god, an idea. It seems to me that if we leave our faith on such an abstract level, then it is unlikely to defeat the suggestive power that virtuous acts can merit eternal life. After all, we would expect that from a just god! Yet as Pascal reminds us, the god of the philosophers is not the God of Abraham, Isaac, and Jacob. The Bible tells us nothing about why Abraham would have "deserved" to be elected father of many nations. Likewise, it is never suggested in the scriptures that Mary "deserved" to become the Mother of God. Both were chosen because of their faith, not due to any acts that could be attributed to their human will and nature. Once we live with Christ in a state of grace, we receive the gift of perseverance also to overcome the temptation of Pelagius and Adam Smith.

Only a real, direct encounter with Christ can help us avoid thinking in these Pelagian ways. It is here where one can learn the most from the great mystics of the Christian tradition, who show us that nobody who looks and reflects on the image of Christ being brutally flagellated and pierced through hands and feet can remain untouched unless he has a heart of stone. It is here that the mystery lies. God did not spare his Son from suffering and descending into hell, as the Creed confirms.

If we have seen God's human face in Jesus Christ, we do not have to be afraid and look to God as the unpredictable divine force; rather, we will see him as the immensurable source of mercy and love. By making his suffering our own, especially by offering our own pains up to him, we enter the profound mystery that the great things in life are all beyond purchase and that friendship with God is the greatest among them. By becoming Christlike, we are transformed and God is no longer a being alien to us, "for in him we live and move and have our being" (Acts 17:28).

THE GOD OF
THUNDER

As a German, I hate it when my schedule is interrupted. A leaking roof that doesn't let me sleep at night or a sudden job emergency that overthrows my vacation plans—such are my nemeses. Thus, to think of God as somebody who interrupts my life is not only challenging but also highly inconvenient. Is he the God who asked Abraham to leave his home and sacrifice his son and the God who interrupted the career of Saul the Pharisee and persecutor of Christians? Do I believe that he can enter my life like thunder and lightning, asking me to give my life to him? The vitality of my faith depends on how I view him as God.

In 1960, Walter Miller published the novel *A Canticle for Leibowitz*. It is set in the future United States after a devastating nuclear war has destroyed much of civilization, including all the great libraries. Some knowledge has survived, but scientific information is particularly rudimentary and fragmentary. Some bits and pieces of books on modern physics escaped the mushroom clouds, but their frame of reference is gone. The readers of the future have no idea who Isaac Newton was nor what brought Albert Einstein to question established physics. I have the impression that something similar has happened to how we think of God. We have a rough idea of God but have lost the context in which God belongs. We have cut God off as the life support of our faith life. Instead, God has become a bloodless idea that doesn't warm us or fulfill us.

Real and Not Made Up

If our view of God has changed so much, could the problem be that we have made God a concept? Did we suck the life out of faith when we began reasoning about God? Let's not delude ourselves: God is a person and a reality, not a fancy word. Every one of us uses concepts; without concepts we would be lost in the world. Our mind creates them when it encounters reality. "Forest," for instance, is a concept, as is "number." If we did not have concepts, our words would be merely names for things and we could not do real science because every encounter with a thing would be different. We need concepts to describe reality, and it is worth thinking about how we acquire and use them. After all, we have active minds and are not just human computers.

Our reason needs concepts to work with, and it matters what our concepts are and where they originate. If our concepts do not correspond to a reality, they are fictitious. They may sound lovely, but they do not grasp any reality. In particular, it is important to have the right concept of God, which is so important that the Gospel of John begins by reminding us of this truth: the Incarnate Son of God has revealed the Father (Jn 1:18). Without Jesus, we would never have the right concept of God. Certainly, it is a concept circumscribed by our human limitations, but, nevertheless, as Christians we believe that we understand some basic facts about God through revelation.

The Church reminds us to use reason to further enlighten our faith and to make it intelligible. We cannot stand still but have to move, have to discover insights into the mystery of God ourselves. If we wander with holy scripture and reason toward God, we are well equipped for our journey. Then we realize that we have been searching for the right "concept" of God, not just in thought but in thought and prayer.

The way previous generations have understood God has been destroyed. Today, most people tend to think about God as we think about moral choices. We express our opinions about God, such as "God is universal and forgiving love. Out of love he created human beings. Therefore all humans will go to heaven after their death because God forgives everybody. Hell is just a fiction." Although such conclusions follow from the premises, what we no longer see is that the premises are hardly ever based on reason but simply on somebody's fancy.

Instead of basing statements about God on good logical arguments, such as those posed by St. Thomas Aquinas, St. Anselm, and others, many published views about God today are opinion pieces. They are mostly generated by emotions and experiences and never tried by reason. As a theologian, I ask *why* God is love and *what* forgiveness entails and *whether* it can be bestowed on someone who does not ask for forgiveness. I look for reasons, not opinions.

Questioning concepts about God is a *rational* enterprise. However, if one challenges someone else's views today, many people will not respond with reason; they will instead try to morally undercut the one who questions them. Unfortunately, this approach has become endemic even to the guild of professional theologians. They respond with a value statement: "Because I believe forgiveness and love are the highest values, I hold this position." This statement, of course, entails an attack on the person who asked for reason. He is now portrayed as a person for whom love and forgiveness are *not* the highest values, although he never doubted these values. And there is no explanation of how God's justice might fit into the whole picture. Such attacks, sometimes subtle, sometimes openly vicious, have become commonplace. As a consequence, many sincere thinkers have withdrawn from serious dialogue about God and have left the field to pseudoacademics, who sell their opinions about the divine without adhering to the most basic principles of logic and Christian tradition.

The concept of God has become something that anybody can say anything about without having to defend it. If somebody criticizes my account, I can simply brush him off with a statement such as "You obviously do not share my values" or "My position is the most compassionate for the poor and marginalized." Suddenly I have painted the person who wanted to examine the rationale behind my arguments as a supporter of societal oppressors and an enemy of the poor, because he asked a question. That is how any serious search for truth ends—and I have seen it happen countless times.

The question is, How did we get here? Why can't we talk rationally about God or any other objective truth claims anymore? I believe there are several reasons. The philosopher Alasdair MacIntyre provides us with one of them in his classic book *After Virtue*.[1] He exposes the pitfalls of modern moral philosophy and maintains that a movement called emotivism is the ultimate reason for this development.

Although "emotivism" sounds awfully complicated, it really isn't. Emotivism means that something is good or bad because our emotions tell us it is good or bad, not because of a quality or action it possesses. I "feel" that my neighbor is right in putting up a fence: such a stance gives no reasons; nobody can argue with my feelings. Moreover, emotivists believe that one can judge actions only according to their outcome; if their outcome gives us pleasure, they are good. If not, they are bad. If smoking a joint relaxes me, it can't be bad. If premarital sex doesn't hurt anybody, it can't be bad. As a consequence, emotivists believe that there can never be objective moral standards. They begin to get into serious trouble, however, when faced with statements such as "Rape is always evil."

This philosophy of whim has already taken over the media and our universities, and more and more parents have succumbed to it, too. Because there is no objective standard for good and evil in emotivism and nothing is good in itself, anything can be declared moral as long as one "feels" it is right. Blogs, the newspaper, and television are full of emotivists. They have become legion. They legitimize bad behavior with statements such as "I felt it was the right thing to do." Because an emotivist rejects rational criteria (such as objective values, natural law, etc.) as standards, he is always right: whatever topic he chooses to speak about, he is always right. (It is a bit different in the *hard* sciences, though!) You cannot argue with someone who "feels" he is right and does not submit to rational standards.

Feelings Can Be Deceiving

If feelings control our lives, we easily arrive at the notion that they are the true core of our conscience. No wonder so many pastors and theologians try to sell us this notion, too, even though it is incredibly dangerous.

Every semester I remind my students: "I do care for you as human beings and for your feelings. But papers are written to demonstrate your thinking skills, and that's why I don't accept 'I feel' as a valid argument." More puzzled faces. Many, if not most, of them probably grew up pampered by teachers and parents reiterating the mantra, "Whatever you feel is right." At some point in class, inevitably, I ask my students to consider this consequence: Hitler felt right to kill six million Jews. Was he right in doing so? Was it okay that he followed his conscience?

The theological tradition has an answer that is called *invincible ignorance*. If one does not form one's conscience to understand the difference between good and evil, one becomes ignorant of the most basic moral laws. So Hitler followed his conscience, or more accurately, the absence of a conscience. For an emotivist, however, there is no standard for morality. It does not make a difference whether you are St. Teresa of Calcutta or Joseph Stalin. Certainly, most emotivists would not accept that premise and would try to explain that it is always bad to inflict harm on other people; but when you ask them on what they base this insight, many—if they are honest—fall silent. They have no foundation other than their feelings, which can never be imposed on everyone. You cannot force your enemy to feel like you!

There is a reason why I have spent so much time on this topic. Emotivism penetrates our entire society and injects its poison into all our value systems. It eats away at everything. Feelings govern our attitudes toward our neighbors and God. As a result, we cast away virtue and natural law because they don't feel right. The idea that we should subject thoughts and feelings to reason, Church tradition, and holy scripture seems laughable at best and dangerous at worst. We have become "whimsical Christians," to borrow a phrase from the great lay theologian Dorothy L. Sayers. Our concept of who God is is made to fit our current mood.

More Than a Rule Book

The erosion that Alasdair MacIntyre speaks about did not begin in the twentieth century. It was the fruit of a long process that originated, as I have said, in the Enlightenment. During the eighteenth century, sources of authority were questioned, obscure language was rejected, and scientific discovery advanced—all these are laudable things. Yet something else began at that time: God was no longer an object of lively faith but was seen only to fulfill certain roles and functions. This is why, when that notorious critic of organized religion, Voltaire, was asked whether he wished his servant to be religious, he answered, "Of course, because then it's less likely he will steal from me!"

God also then fulfilled the role of making the philosophically uneducated morally responsible. A philosopher such as Voltaire, of course, did not need to believe in such a chimera to be moral (or so he said). Without belief in God, Voltaire claimed, illiterate people would cheat, disobey the law, and break up their family ties. Many theologians bought into this apologetic strategy, yet religion paid a heavy price for invoking God as the *stabilizer* of society. First, it was soon assumed that as long as I am well educated I do not need God, especially if I view the Bible merely as a moral rule book. Second, faith was identified with hypocrisy, meaning that we just pretend it tells the truth about the world and God.

From this discourse, modern atheists drew the conclusion that Christian "morality" is redundant. After all, one now has reason as an infallible moral guide and doesn't need the "rule book of the dumb," as some eighteenth-century philosophers called the Bible. They held that it had become impossible for any reasonable person to accept the Bible as a moral guide. I actually think there is a lot of value in this criticism, because it reminds us that we should not teach our children a Christian morality that simply functions to stabilize society but rather give them *reasons* for our Christian moral standards and outline their intelligibility. Is this easy? Certainly not. But let's take the example of sexuality as just one sphere of human morality: it is a challenging enterprise to prepare children for the world and to educate them about their sexuality, but if we as parents do not do it, then the secular world will and in ways that contradict our faith. We cannot expect religious educators to do all the work—the most important formation falls on us.

Beware of Humanist Religion

Sometimes I wonder how many Christians and even pastors teach this sort of Enlightenment philosophy instead of true Christian theology. "If you believe in God, you will be more successful and you will be a good person." This sounds awfully close to the movement called the prosperity gospel, in which God is used as a key to personal success and financial well-being. Instead of being an end in himself as goodness, beauty, and truth, God is a means to achieve earthly goods.

This turns prayer into something like self-affirmation and self-training. It certainly is not communication with a living and active God. Rather, it is like a five-year-old chatting with herself in the mirror. This distorted image of Christianity is what atheists have in mind when they encourage others to give up their faith. Such faith, they say, is mere hypocrisy. Why would anybody need a God for self-affirmation? Why the act?

Indeed, many modern atheists see the point far better than most Christians. They understand that we have replaced the God who sends his Son to save us with an idol of our own making.

Because Christianity was for a long time the reigning religion and supported, often unconsciously, the idea of God as a stabilizing force for society, societal hypocrisy is now attributed to our faith. And in all honesty, we have failed to withhold ammunition from our critics. We have provided them with the misconduct of priests and religious, financial irregularities, transgressions of self-appointed Catholic leaders, and also our own cold hearts. With great delight these scandals are brought out into the open, but one easily forgets that, because the Church consists of fallen human beings, such transgressions are to be expected! This does not ease their egregiousness, however, because as people of faith we should be better.

Critics often charge Christians with being unable to justify their moral standards. It is irrational, they say, to believe that an embryo is a human person only because the Bible says so. It is illogical to remain chaste before marriage only because the Bible tells you to. Indeed it would be. Yet no serious Catholic would say such things. The point is that reason *and* revelation tell us that a human being in a womb is a person, even if a very small one, and reason and revelation also tell us that sex has to do with responsibility and personal maturity.

I want to make sure that I get this point across: when we defend our faith just by pointing to an authority, we do not convince others or even ourselves. By defending moral standards in our communities with truisms (premarital sex is morally wrong because it is wrong), we in fact advance the cause of the enemies of religion. We need to be able to express at least some arguments from reason—for ourselves, so that we grow deeper in faith, but also in order to be disciples and witnesses in a world that is deaf to the Good News. I learned this from observing my own kids: they ask, very directly, questions such as, "Why do we as Catholics do this?" And children realize immediately if you don't have an answer; they deserve from us more than an appeal to parental authority. We should not be afraid of explaining the reasoning of the Church—nobody's perfect. None of us is Thomas Aquinas or Augustine, but if we expose ourselves to the teachings of the Church, live by them and interact with others who believe the same, we will have enough to answer. Most importantly, the best defense of the faith is living it joyfully!

If not us, who can show the world that believers are not intellectually disabled? By using reason, we take a defense that the Bible recommends to us (1 Pt 3:15), and we reject emotivism and the onslaught on objective moral standards. If one does not know in the heat of a discussion exactly how to articulate the argument, the best way is always to listen and to ask the opponent what Socrates used to ask: "Why?" And never, ever lead a discussion with your conclusion!

Remember: reducing Christianity to a form of morality is a dangerous business. Our faith entails moral rules, but these are just means to an end—namely, to transforming the human person, of becoming transformed in Christ. Equating religion with morality seems to be the biggest burden the Enlightenment thinkers left us. It weighs not only on philosophers and theologians but also seemingly on society as a whole. If religion was just a construct of what to do and what not to do, then Auguste Comte, the early nineteenth-century father of modern atheism, was right. He claimed that science was the only enlightened way to look at the world and that all religions are leftovers from primitive stages of humanity. Comte argued that in the first stage, humans divinized nature and natural events. In the second stage, they began to reason about them and explained them with the help of philosophy. But in the third stage, Comte claimed, people are able to give up theological prejudices and use science to explain everything. If religion is needed only to tame brutes, then the civilized human being of the twenty-first century needs only science to become "good."

However, Comte realized that even with science, people would remain self-absorbed narcissists. So he taught that at the third stage of human development, historical religions such as Christianity will have to be replaced with a religion-like "belief" in humanity. Love is the principle of this "religion" and progress is its goal. Love meant for Comte "the subjection of self-interest to social feeling"—in other words, altruistic behavior for what a group "feels" is necessary and good. Such love would bring about order in society and lead to further progress.

The problem with Comte's humanistic religion is that it offers no foundation for morality. If there is no God, there are no absolute standards because there is no absolute goodness and truth. We can only serve what society deems good, and those conventions can easily be turned evil. Even if we acknowledge the humanist position that "whatever advances society is good," there would be no agreed-upon understanding of "good," "advanced," or even "society." After all, Hitler and Stalin wanted to advance humanity in their own perverse ways. Comte anticipated this, and so he appeals to the social feeling or sentiment—whatever society "feels" is right and moral.

This, however, is emotivism on steroids: things do not become good because people agree they are good. Would the practice of selective infanticide on girls (as practiced in ancient China) be moral because a society "feels" and agrees to accept it? Would it be moral if we agreed to euthanize everybody over sixty-five in order to save social security?

What is common to all atheist formulations of "belief in mankind" is that values are based on *societal agreement and utility*, and those can substantially change. Theologies, when they are infected by Enlightenment thought, tend to functionalize God. They (mostly unconsciously) follow Comte and Voltaire into this trap. Once caught in the spiderweb of moralism, as we can call this perverted version of Christian thought, Jesus becomes a moral teacher, the Bible a book with "signposts," and the magisterium of the Church a "helpful guide." God becomes a nice buddy, a friend, but he cannot be a savior. He certainly cannot be a judge because ultimately it is our feelings that make actions good or bad. Our feelings decide whether the image we paint of God is true or not. Such theology is comforting like velvet and smooth like honey. However, when theology is not clothed in the tattered robes of the carpenter, drenched in his blood, and a scandal to look at, it is not from God but man-made.

The Walmart Church

Smooth Christianity is, of course, much nicer to look at: it has no edges and dark spots; it is advertised as the place where you "feel welcome." To be honest, I always think of a Walmart greeter when a pastor uses that phrase, and I think it points to a real problem in our churches: we focus too much on feeling. This danger was recognized a century ago by one of the most unjustly slandered popes of all time, St. Pius X. During his pontificate (1903–1914), a number of theologians began to overemphasize the role of religious experience, and the pontiff feared that this would lead to an erosion of the content of faith. He believed that emotional experience of the divine might replace the content of faith and the need to form one's conscience and mind according to the teachings of the Church and holy scripture. The late pontiff called this trend "modernism." Pope Pius X was so afraid of modernism infiltrating the Church that he also suspected orthodox theologians, who argued for a different style in theology or modern exegesis. There is no doubt that he was far too harsh in his punishment of dissenters, but I believe that he rightly identified a danger to reason and the faith.

Unfortunately, especially since the 1960s, the emphasis on religious feeling has increased dramatically. Now, however, it hides behind such catchy phrases as "the sense of the faithful" or "the voice of the faithful" or "the real-world experience of the people in the pews." Traditional doctrines and concepts of God are questioned because they do not fit into the individual experience and agenda of theologians. Since they know they have to give reasons for their dissent, they disguise their emotions by appealing to the "experience of the faithful."

People who have been marginalized by Church authorities are interviewed, case studies that show Church hypocrisy are presented, and people who feel they are not listened to or taken seriously by bishops and popes are cited. Such appeals ought to call to mind Comte's "social feeling," or the feeling of the masses. Even Comte's principle of love is universally invoked by such theologians when they argue, for example, that because God is love, the Church should give up canon law or stop teaching its supposedly rigid morality.

When we are asked to define love and to explain the relationship between love, justice, mercy, and grace as an undeserved gift, something interesting happens: our masks fall off. People say, "We believe love to be the most important attribute of God," or "Mercy is the core of the Christian faith," often combined with the slur, "and you obviously do not hold these values to be important." It is clear what happens here; one does not answer the request for rational clarification but simply appeals to an opinion based on emotion. We cannot reasonably argue with people in such situations. We cannot communicate with those who view (or better, emote) their opinions as the last and infallible judgment on a certain matter—they are emotivists.

Theologians and philosophers have passed on this attitude to us in the pews, especially through catechesis or the lack thereof. I have heard from theological educators that they value the "experience of feeling welcome" over a personal transformation in Christ. The idea is that people should be freed from an outdated concept of God as vengeful and rigid. Nobody asked, however, whether this was really true—whether anyone really taught such a rigid and revengeful God—or whether certain aspects of Christian doctrine were unjustly overemphasized, which is a different issue altogether.

Opening up any Catholic textbook of the 1950s makes clear that God was never portrayed as many liberal theologians claim. But, it must be said, certain aspects of God's justice and law *were* overemphasized, whereas the teaching on Christian transformation and mercy was often neglected. That is why Hildebrand wrote his masterful *Transformation in Christ* in the 1940s and August Adam his *Primacy of Love* in 1932. Yet instead of continuing their work after the Second Vatican Council and deepening catechesis, theological educators replaced content with feeling. This was not a Catholic phenomenon alone but is almost universally true of all Christian denominations.

Over the next two decades, the Church desired to be modern and to engage with the modern world, in which feelings had become infallible. By making people feel welcome, Catholics set out to create an atmosphere of safety to which people would return with joy. We seem to have believed that this would stop an exodus of churchgoers. One could call this the "Walmart mentality," since at Walmart we are greeted with a big, cordial welcome. Just like Walmart, however, in churches where this happened, the idea of God was also changed according to season, supply, and demand. Churchgoers no longer went to Mass because they worshiped the one true God, who saved them and called them to everlasting union with him, but because it made them feel good. "I want to get something out of Mass" became a standard expectation. Consequently, priests tried to come up with new ideas for attracting the crowds, just as in a supermarket. Prices, or better yet, expectations of the faithful, were lowered. Every season, new "sales events" were launched, and consequently churchgoers began to expect, as in the consumer world, a never-ending series of gratifying shopping experiences.

Shopping in a store helps us avoid reality. In Walmart church, we find a god who is no longer wild and who never takes us on an adventure—a boring heavenly grandpa who will not cause us any discomfort. I can sit on this god's lap just like on Santa Claus's lap in the mall, tell him my wishes, receive a smile and pat on the back—he makes me feel good. Of such a god we do not expect much; there is no reason to search in the depths of my soul to bring my desires and needs to him. Why should I pray to a Jesus who is just "a symbol for God's love for humanity" and the "greatest teacher of human solidarity"? If god is no longer God, praying is a waste of time.

By equating religion and morality, Enlightenment thought has brought a deadly disease to theology. It reduces the Christian life to a set of rules and eliminates the need of a personal encounter with the triune God.

The Jewish philosopher Martin Buber once said that all real life is "meeting" somebody else. Unfortunately, we are sometimes content with an unreal God, just hearing his echoes in moral rules. We do not know why they exist or that they are means to a higher end—namely, to meet God face-to-face. The Church was unfortunately at times complicit in this endeavor by emphasizing the "role" of God for society. Afraid it would lose influence and possibly many members, it went along with Enlightenment thought and preached that without God society would fall apart. In doing so, it lost the message that every baptized person is called to become another Christ.

Selling God through a welcoming atmosphere is repeating the same mistake—adapting Christianity to the world instead of fermenting the world with the Gospel of Christ. The God of Abraham, Isaac, and Jacob has become the god of Walmart. A faith with content, truth claims, and commitment has been replaced by a religion of fuzzy feelings. Far too many catechists and theologians have made millions of Catholics believe that rational standards, tradition, and scripture do not matter as much as the "experience of the faithful." This experience, derived from a wide array of intellectual and emotional spheres, as the saints knew, has been widely reduced to emotional reaction. Thus, some justify their actions by saying they feel such and such is right; one cannot have a rational conversation with such a person because he is an emotivist. For such a person, true and false have lost their meaning, and his god might make you feel welcome but he will not save, because he is not real.

THE GOD OF TERROR

I distinctly remember my grandfather telling me as a teenager, "We never read the Old Testament in school. We were told not to." I assume my grandfather must have had either a bad teacher or one who was overly cautious. Indeed, many people still buy into the lie that the Old Testament God and the New Testament God are entirely different. That is, in the Old Testament, God is presented as vengeful and rigid, whereas in the New Testament, God is all-loving and not at all concerned about being obeyed. Nothing could be further from the truth. The two work together to reveal God's character, as Jesus himself showed us by treating the Hebrew Bible, what Christians know as the Old Testament, as the very words of God.

Beyond the Literal Meaning of the Bible

In the 1600s, new scientific discoveries began to shed doubt on the Bible's account of the world's age. When Christian missionaries returned from China and shared their findings that Chinese culture was older than the Bible's timeline, European scholars were shocked. Yet they soon realized that the biblical chronology had to be understood not literally but allegorically. There could not be a contradiction between the truth of history and the truth of the Bible. It was also in this period that theologians began to realize that the Old Testament wasn't a book of science.

This was nothing new. In the third century, Origen, one of the greatest theological minds of all time, had demonstrated that the Old Testament contained passages that contradicted science or Christian beliefs. If read literally, such passages would portray God as vindictive and demanding from his people genocide and infanticide (for example, Psalm 137). Origen also taught that the creation accounts of Genesis, chapters one and two, which are so often used to ridicule Christians, are *not* to be taken literally: "Who is so silly as to believe that God, after the manner of a farmer, 'planted a paradise eastward of Eden,' and set in it a visible and palpable 'tree of life' of such a sort that anyone who tasted its fruit with his bodily teeth would gain life?"[1]

Instead, Origen and the Church Fathers, including St. Augustine, explained that there were ways of interpreting conflicts between the biblical text, the faith of the Church, *and* scientific evidence. Since the Old Testament was the inspired Word of God, it was true, but when it contradicted other truths, such as Christian doctrine, it had to be interpreted in consistency with them.

For example, should Psalm 137 be taken literally that God was enticing the Israelites to kill the babies of the Amalekites and smash their heads against a stone? Was God really encouraging infanticide? This would contradict the Christian doctrine of God as love and compassion and justice. Consequently, the Fathers interpreted such passages as metaphorical and thus made them consistent with their belief system. The babes were not innocent humans but an image for the evil offspring we produce—our sins—and the stone against which they should be smashed was the "rock" whom the master builders had rejected, Jesus Christ.

The task of a biblical interpreter was then to find out what passages had to be taken literally and which could not. Augustine explained that if the literal understanding of a Bible passage conflicts with what the Church and the reader believe about God and morality, then the reader has to interpret the text as an image or as a figure of speech.[2] This way of reading scripture "allegorically," in which concrete things and events really mean something more abstract (such as the example from Psalm 137), was discredited by Enlightenment thinkers in the 1700s.

Flattening Holy Writ

In 1670, Baruch Spinoza began to disseminate the theory that there was only one legitimate way of reading the Bible—namely, as a piece of literature. If it was to be read like Homer's writings or a newspaper, however, one had to subtract everything supernatural from it. For Spinoza, the Bible was simply a book with a message created by very imaginative humans, not the Word of God. History and knowledge of Hebrew grammar provide us, in his theory, with the only necessary keys to unlock scripture. There was no longer a need for a church or synagogue to help explain the holy book. Moreover, beginning with Spinoza, scripture was not to be read with the understanding that God—who could not contradict himself—was the ultimate author. Instead of viewing the text as part of a three-dimensional puzzle, the followers of Spinoza now argued we would have to see the text as a one-dimensional enterprise.

The Bible became a text that had to be taken literally *only*, and inconsistencies and claims of falsity were just that and nothing more. The consequence was that faith in the Old Testament as a divinely inspired book was shattered. How could God reveal himself by asking the Israelites to commit genocide (Dt 7:1–2), by punishing the innocent Job, or by establishing a national, tribal religion? With the elimination of allegorical readings, the Old Testament became a book Christians were increasingly ashamed of. It was brushed off as representing a primitive stage of religion from which Christianity had developed. It could still offer a few good stories regarding moral development but not much more.

Welfare but No Adventure

It is quite understandable that Enlightenment thinkers and modern scientists replaced the mysterious God of old who spoke in some-times obscure ways that had to be taken allegorically with an under-standable God who speaks as clearly as a scientist and is as amiable as a car salesman. After all, we want to understand what God says. But unlike previous generations, we do not have the patience to listen; we want to know right away instead of contemplating the Word of God—"going pregnant" with it, as some saints describe it.

God has become, John Crowe Ransom stated in 1931, "the embodiment mostly of the principle of social benevolence and phys-ical welfare." I think that is a pretty good summary of what many believe today: God is good for social justice and welfare. Of course, this plain truth sometimes hides behind a more elaborate way of describing it. A theologian could, for example, say that becoming Christlike means becoming altruistic and concerned with the com-mon good. Christianity is then no more than a tool to form our conscience and to aspire to a more humanitarian world.[3] Certainly, faith forms our conscience, but does it do no more than develop our aspirations? Is it nothing more than a club promoting universal welfare?

No, these theologians would respond, because Christianity also makes us moral. God wants to educate our moral selves, and faith is leading us in this direction. Everything that exists is the play-house of this school of morality. The created world is brought into being by God as a lawgiver and engineer. All that God does is serve humanity. That, of course, fits with the idea many have of modern science: it is good as far as it is useful. God is the superscientist on a cloud high above who arranged everything so that humanity can comfortably exist.

Do we not see that such a view of God is utterly deficient— and really just a projection of our needs? Why did we "tame" the wild God, domesticating him to be a heavenly social worker? Is it because we do not want an unpredictable God? The gods of the ancient Greeks remained unpredictable and mysterious as was the God of the Bible and of the Church Fathers. In stark contrast, the modern God of Christianity is predictable, like the outcome of a known experiment. His ways are scientifically discoverable (scientific laws) as are his intentions (human benevolence).

In this new worldview, God looks like a scientist who is busy with humanity alone. As a scientist would never interfere with an experiment, so God would not interfere with his creation. Thus, God becomes a lawgiver and lifeless principle who runs the universe like a CEO. In philosophy, such a view is called *deism*. A deist theology was much easier to reconcile with the New Testament than with the Old. One could easily read Jesus' healings as therapeutic events and explain supernatural occurrences such as miracles. But one could not do so with the Old Testament. If taken literally, the God of the Old seemed just too unpredictable and contrary to create a stable universe with eternal laws. After all, he had changed his mind several times and found it necessary first to enter a covenant with Noah, then with Abraham, and then with Moses.

Moses himself was an embarrassment. A man who reportedly killed a guard out of anger over his treatment of his fellow Israelites could not possibly be regarded as the greatest prophet. And were the Ten Commandments not just human laws that he learned during his time in Egypt and were thus merely imported from a more highly

developed religion? Was it not unreasonable to believe that God
fed the Israelites with daily miracles of bread and flesh from heaven
for forty years? Many even went so far as to doubt the historicity of
Moses himself and of the exodus as a real event.

Trashing the Ten Commandments

Lying behind this embarrassment about Moses, but mostly unac-
knowledged, were two philosophical ideas of the late 1800s. The first
had been developed by the German Friedrich Nietzsche. For him, the
Old Testament bore witness to religion's enslavement of the "stron-
gest" persons, who were condemned to a life of mediocrity through
the taming of their energies and their subjugation to the burden of
a "slave morality," as he called the Ten Commandments. Although
most Christians rejected Nietzsche, many unconsciously accepted
his main idea—namely, that humanity was better off without the
ballast of the Old Testament.

The second idea behind the disparagement of Moses was a
renewed racist anti-Semitism. Indeed, one cannot write the history of
modern theology without acknowledging a strong tendency toward
anti-Semitism and thus of a vindictive aggression toward the Jewish
people and their holy book. Especially in Nazi Germany, Christians (in fact, a majority of the Lutheran and Evangelical Churches)
embraced the idea that Jesus wanted to overcome his Jewishness and
that one could be Christian without the Old Testament. The "German
Christians," as they called themselves, believed that Christianity was
a set of beliefs that enabled them to become superior to other races.
God served a function and was predictable. This is not far from the
contemporary view of a God who "makes us happy and prosperous."

Rediscovering the Mystery

How do we turn the tide and return to the true God? The moment
we realize how infinitely boring such a tame and predictable god

is, we have stepped on the road to recovery. Try a simple test: Ask a group of children or teenagers whether they find God exciting. Perhaps they have never thought about that, so ask who God is for them and watch their expressions. Can you detect passion and enthusiasm or rather the attitude, "I have to go to church because of my parents"? My encounters with students suggest that they find the God of the Bible boring—because their parents and teachers never showed much passion but also because their questions about how faith and reason go together were never seriously answered. A simple "You have to believe" gives the impression of irrationality. We can do better! But the other extreme is that we try to explain faith like algebra, robbing it of its mystery. We have to find a good middle ground. Since I have already talked about how to approach God with reason, here I would like to show how we can rediscover the mystery we have lost. How can we rediscover the God of the Old Testament, what the German Protestant theologian Rudolf Otto called the mystery of *The Holy*?[4]

Otto was fed up with the lifelessness of established theology. He realized that German Lutherans focused too much on God's rational side—his attributes, eternal decrees, and existence—and underrated the experiential, "irrational" side of God. "Irrational" in his eyes did not mean contradicting logic but rather referred to a sphere that was beyond the grasp of human language. Otto lamented that a faith focused on the rationally accessible sides of God, as we described them above with the image of the superscientist or the moral supervisor, would sooner or later wither and lose every true dimension of emotional experience. The Holy, as Otto discovered it in world religions, was never first and foremost "good" or "moral." Instead, the initial response of humans of all times toward encounters with the divine was that the divine was infinitely superior.

We approach this mystery with trembling and fear. The Hebrew Bible calls this the *emat* of God, the fear of God (Ex 23:27).

In English, this experience is encapsulated in the word *awe*. We can grasp a rudimentary version of this when we watch a horror movie and an uncanny feeling comes over us. As a scary story can give us goosebumps, so can God, but only because he comes unexpectedly and because his presence so utterly diminishes our own. Nothing nice makes us tremble! Mary Poppins and Mickey Mouse make us laugh and smile. But they do not elicit the feeling we experience when we encounter a work of art that brings us in contact with our own heart as it touches the transcendent world. It should be obvious that awe is utterly different from the superficial feel-good response to an entertaining movie or shallow theology.

If we begin reading the Hebrew Bible through Otto's lenses, new dimensions begin to open up. We realize that the biblical narratives are attempts to put into words the experience of the awesome God who by definition escapes our conceptual language. If this is our key, then suddenly the harshest narratives of the Bible begin to make sense and lose their appalling coarseness.

The mystery of God that makes us tremble, the anger of God, is one of the best examples to demonstrate this point. How often does a twenty-first-century reader have the thought that the God of the Israelites was very similar to a human person: unpredictable and emotional, such as when he struck humans without reasonable measure in Noah's flood or all the firstborns in the last plague or even when he was wrestling with Jacob? Yet ancient readers did not find these accounts contradicted the goodness and beauty of God, because they were not interested in such compatibility questions. For them, the wonder of God, the awe-inspiring experience of the divine, was the center of the story. This awe was described with the nearest analogy they had at hand—the "irrational," unpredictable, unreasonable, odd behavior of fellow humans! What other images do we have than those from our own lives? The God who was so described was the ultimate majesty, as Otto writes, but not full of contradictions.

Another "irrational" characteristic of the divine is its energy. This energy embodies vivacity and passion, especially in God's will-power, yet all these aspects contradict a mere philosophical concept of God—they sound too human. As Otto shows, philosophers have not understood that the authors of the Bible were aware of this more than two thousand years ago but used such descriptions as embodiments of an idea, to describe the unspeakable, mysterious, lively, passionate side of God!

The last characteristic of the divine mystery Otto discovered is the "utter otherness." When we encounter God, his complete otherness makes us shiver—he has no beginning and no end, no cause, is neither in space nor in time, is omniscient, all-powerful, and so on. His attributes inebriate our reasoning faculties. But what is the content of this mystery? Otto calls this the fascinating side of the divine, the qualities that attract and enchant us. It is this side that mystics of all religions describe in their desire to be united with the godhead, in the incredible longing for fulfillment and bliss. But only after reflecting on the experience of trembling and fascination does the divine begin to be seen as good and valuable, as the source of all values, especially by devaluing ourselves in comparison with it.

Trembling and Enchanting

This is a truth that many have forgotten. If I have not experienced the divine mystery as the one that makes me tremble and enchants me at the same time, I will most likely never feel the smallness of human existence and acknowledge the great gift of grace. *Sin* becomes a word without meaning, because without love, the true love that is God, there is no sin. I have to experience to some degree the divine love in order to grasp how much disorder and evil sin brings into the world. Martin Luther knew this when he said, "Sin but believe even stronger!" He did not mean that a saintly person should commit sins but that the more a person loves God, the more sinful she will find herself. Most churches today, however, have given in to sentimentalism. God is a moral supervisor who does not excite or attract. He sits like Confucius on the altar and teaches us how to live. He gives us guidelines like a well-meaning grandpa. It is this destruction of the mystery of God that has blinded us to sin because we no longer acknowledge grace as a life-transforming force.

First and foremost, (unfortunately) theologians are to blame for this. Too many have been silent about how prayer and awe change us. Through this silence, religion has been flattened—robbed of its third dimension, so to speak. Rediscovering the side of God that reason cannot grasp, the mystery that enchants and frightens us, doesn't mean contradicting and despising logic, but rather involves accepting the wisdom to know how far logic can bring us. We cannot attempt to comprehend this side of the divine, but we can, as Otto also showed, try to describe some of its effects on us and thus come to a better understanding of the elements of the mysterious, also in order to counter those who preach a God of arbitrariness. This sense of the incomprehensible God is especially present in the works of Martin Luther and the Pietist tradition, but it is also present among the Catholic mystics such as St. Teresa of Avila, St. John of the Cross, and St. Francis de Sales. If we do not take seriously the feeling that breaks forth from our soul, a sense for the Holy, or when we reduce it to an impulse, God becomes an object for academics. Pressed between two book covers, his spirit is confined to solving moral riddles and philosophical questions, no longer allowed to set the soul ablaze.

Perhaps the most dramatic effect of our flattened understanding of God is the redefinition of sin. Sin becomes a category of wrongdoings that one can rationalize. It loses all connection to our spiritual health. When I commit a sin, I usually find reasons afterward to ease my guilty conscience; I find excuses. The bad actions are seen as no more than a stain on an otherwise clean shirt. It is therefore enough to brush the stain off. After all, one can wear a shirt even if it has a slight discoloration here and there.

Christian theology, however, has never used such imagery. In fact, sin is a destructive moment in our lives. When I teach second-graders, I usually rip a piece of paper apart and explain: "This is our relationship with God. It is ruptured. The one piece of paper is us, the other is God. There is nothing that brings the two sides back together except some really good tape—and that is Jesus Christ." If we understand sin as the breaking of a friendship or covenant and leave the unbiblical imagery of the stained shirt behind, we will regain the dimension of sin that gives us back the God that touches our innermost heart.

Then we recapture the God whom we take seriously enough to heal our iniquities and to whom we can come without masks. When we encounter the real God, he can be our physician and divine therapist who knows our needs better than we know ourselves. This therapist is not there to give in to our demands and make us feel happy but to heal the wounds of our souls, to purge us from our sins and fears. To call this doctor-friend "nice" would degrade his love to the attentiveness of a modern-day health-care professional. At the same time, this God is mysterious and unpredictable—not because God is whimsical as we are, changing his mind, but because we are unable to grasp God's essence, his ideas and plans, or as St. Thomas Aquinas frequently put it, because our finite minds are like owls staring into the midday sun, unable to comprehend infinite brightness.[5]

Over the last decades, much has been done to help Christians rediscover this God of the Old Testament, the God of Jesus Christ. Numerous commentaries of the Church Fathers are now available that allow a reading of the Hebrew Bible in harmony with faith and reason, and of course, there are many resources that make use of the prayer book of the Old Testament, the Psalms. Yet it remains a constant challenge to face the mystery that enchants us and makes us tremble.

THE GOD OF SURRENDER

sn't it interesting that we immediately grasp the difference between liking and loving? I like colleagues, but I love my family. Deep down in our hearts, we seem to know what love is. Wouldn't we be shocked if we overheard a mother say to her child in kindergarten, "I like you," while her kid utters, "I love you"? It is only when we are asked to define love that we begin to stutter. Nevertheless, we should ask this question, because it seems to influence our understanding of God.

The Inflation of Love

Sigmund Freud, the father of psychoanalysis, once remarked that our times—he died in the 1930s—have become careless in using the word *love*. I think he is still right. We say we "love" all kinds of things, and we never stop to think how we use this important word. After all, it is love that all humans are aiming at—shouldn't we be careful not to use it in inflationary ways?

Love involves affection. It happens to us. We fall in love with a piece of art, a landscape, or a person because we find her or it "enchanting." Affection and passion describe the sensuous aspect of love. But love also implies the concept of choosing. I choose to love this person and not that person—one of the Latin words for love, *diligere*, is actually derived from the verb "to choose."

Love is an act of the will, a surrender to the other. This means that loving is something that happens in our mind, with our will, and that has a personal quality. Therefore, there can be, as psychoanalyst Erich Fromm has postulated, an "art of loving": only if I make love the highest goal, follow it with perseverance and patience, will I become a master of loving.

The Difference between Nice and Love

But let's go back to love and like. We can like people, and if I am honest, there are far more people I like than I love. And that is good and normal. Why? Love always means personal engagement with the core of another person, and we simply cannot do that with a lot of people on a serious level.

Might this be a grave reason to doubt the possibility of Jesus' command to love one another? Yes and no. If we understand love primarily as something that happens to us, it would be impossible to ask it from us. But as I have tried to explain, love is also—even predominantly—an action of the will, and as such, God can require it from us. In our interaction with others, it seems to mean that we should see others as images of God, just like ourselves. Humans are called to be lovers like God himself!

When Jesus requests that we love our enemies, he is not exactly being nice, is he? Such a command goes beyond what one normally requires of others. In fact, historians have showed that Jesus' command (Mt 5:43–48) was the exact opposite of societal expectations in ancient Greek and Roman culture—the milieu in which he was speaking. At that time, it was in fact a moral principle that one should help only one's friends and try in every way to harm one's enemies.[1]

But what does Jesus' command then mean, concretely? Surely not being nice to the people one meets, with the goal that in the end all humans are united as brothers and sisters. This seems to be the kind of humanist ideal Beethoven mused about in the chorus of his Ninth Symphony rather than what Jesus had in mind. Like every other ideal, it remains without concrete actions because it is too abstract. Love for *humanity* will not initiate virtuous behavior or heroism. The Bible does not state that one should love humanity but rather our neighbors and even our enemies. That is the clue here. Enemy and neighbor are humans we encounter, the people in our lives. Christian love has always a concrete object, a "thou," and it is in this regard that it differs from a humanitarian niceness, which remains abstract and without consequences. Christians are called to invite others into the joy of the risen Christ, and "in this joy it becomes even possible to forgive one's enemies."[2]

He Liberated Me Because He Wants Me

The core of love is to call somebody good. When we tell a spouse "I love you," we mean a variety of things, but at the fundamental level we mean to say, "It is good that you exist and that you are with me." The difference from other things that we want or will is that when we love we do not *think*, but we gaze at the beloved. When one loves, one is happy in the moment, in the presence of the beloved.

The Latin translation of Psalm 18:20 states that God has "saved me, because he wanted me" (*salvum me fecit, quoniam voluit me*). God saves us, because he wants us! Yet what does this imply? The newer translations of the Hebrew Bible translate this as "he rescued me because he loves me." When doctors tell us how crucial it is for a newborn to be loved by her parents to survive, then we grasp that in the act of gazing, love is really the key to our existence, and especially to our salvation.[3]

Yet love has another aspect we hardly consider. It vehemently *rejects death*. Some philosophers have found that love is the most powerful force that denies the existence of death, and Gabriel Marcel stated, "To love somebody means to say: You won't die."[4] This sounds like absolute craziness, and Nietzsche had rightly observed that there is always some madness in love. The Judeo-Christian God, however, seems then to be the pinnacle of foolishness when he declares at the beginning of creation, overlooking what he had made, that everything was "very good" (Gn 1:31). By calling creation good, he declares his love and his will to keep it alive. Human love is then, as Josef Pieper deduces, the earthly attempt to imitate the gazing love of God, to participate in the creative love of God. Is such a God nice? I don't think so.[5] The ever so surprising God has woven a pattern into creation that connects us with him in the act of love. Whenever we love, we unearth this secret connection to the divine and to each other; it is a reunion of hitherto-alienated beings.

The Art of Loving God

We like people who are nice, but we do not love them. We like them because they give us a certain pleasant feeling. This pleasantness, however, is momentary and usually weak, and that is why we do not associate it with love. We instinctively know that the value of a relationship with such a person is relatively low. Similarly, when we see God as the being who ensures us a pleasant life, we degrade him to an acquaintance from the school parking lot or the grocery store.

Christians expect from God eternal joy and life—the summit of pleasantness. If we do not love God, then there is a serious disconnect, just like the four-year-old who only "likes" her mother. We have to remember that we are already a temple of the Holy Spirit, at which God gazes every moment of our grace-filled existence in joy.

Instead, however, we expect to be in touch with God only superficially and on Sundays; thus the bond between lover and beloved is broken, and we have become boring Christians who may like God but do not really want God to reshape our body into a temple. We want to be left alone and only get a piece of God when we need it. This makes loving God impossible!

If we apply Fromm's ideas to the life of a Christian, it becomes clear that because we do not make the love of God our highest goal, and because we feel too comfortable in our own little worlds, we undermine the love of God in our lives.

This is an old truth that sociologists have confirmed: people value things higher if they cost more. "Nice" preachers have told generations of Christians that it is easy to live a Christian life and to love God. There is a certain truth in this: it is not rocket science to love God, but most people interpret this message as "I don't have to try very hard." As a consequence, "loving God" has become a commonplace in homilies, talks of theologians, and conversations of parents putting their children to bed. Yet how many talk about the difficulties of loving, the struggles and hardships it entails? How many really assign value to this action of love and make it a priority in life?

"Whoever remains in this love . . . is no longer a mere human"

In order to love, we have to know what love is or at least get a better understanding of its nature. Aristotle gives us a famous definition of love in his *Rhetoric*: "Let loving, then, be defined as wishing for anyone the things which we believe to be good, for his sake but not for our own." He reminds us that often what we believe is love toward our neighbors or enemies is in reality egotistical affection. If we wish somebody well because we fear that if she is doing badly she might turn on us, our wish was centered on us and not the other person. Nevertheless, is Aristotle's definition not too strictly focused on "wishing well"?[6]

Philosophers such as Scheler and Hildebrand thought so and feared that Aristotle marginalized the personal side of love. By talking about goods and wishes, we easily lose sight of the "thou" in our loving. I think, therefore, that Pieper's more basic understanding of love as saying yes to the existence of another person, stating, "It's good that you exist," is a more powerful summary than Aristotle's of what love in a Christian context can mean. When we confirm that it is good that somebody exists, even our greatest enemy, we confirm simultaneously that God has a plan for this person, and we realize that we will be able to turn our aggression and ill will into wishing her God's blessing. Growing in love transforms the human person. Luther knew that when he said, "Whoever remains in this love . . . is no longer a mere human but a god and better than sun and moon, sky and earth . . . because God himself is in him and does such things, which no human nor creature can accomplish."[7]

By saying yes to the other, one answers to the value this person represents, and by doing so one participates in the gift of love. Only when two lovers exchange an unconditional yes to each other do they constitute a unity that transcends their earthly existence and participates in the mystery of the divine life. The result of the complete self-surrender to each other is joy, but it is an effect that comes unintended. It has to be unintended, because if I desired something else besides the beloved—for example, joy—I would be using my beloved to fulfill my needs! It seems to me, however, that that is how many today understand marital love. Nice people get married and seek joy but do not realize it; and because they do not surrender their wishes to each other, they will never experience the gift of love but only a dull shadow of it. They might have some short-lived happiness, but such is a mere façade and has no roots that connect to the transcendent love of God.[8]

Love the Sinner

Yet Christian love also demands that we *hate*—not another person, but sin. When the Church teaches that one should hate sin but love the sinner, it sounds like an impossible task. A nice church and a nice God would pat us on the shoulder and embrace us as we are. Not so the Christian Church. She demands from us that we reject evil but not the person who commits it. On an abstract level this sounds all right, but what does it mean applied to real life?

It demands from us the ability to look beyond a person's evil acts to the core of existence that we share with him, to clear all the stinking rubbish of his life away in order to say, "It is good even that *you* exist!" I think this is much more demanding than anything else Jesus asks of us. Again, it is not an abstract command.

The Bible does not tell us to love sinners universally but the ones we are confronted with; otherwise, we all too easily become indifferent to evil. We let our guard down and become vulnerable. If we decide to love all sinners and to reject sin, we very easily condone the bad behavior of others and sooner or later also downplay their actions. Moreover, it does not take virtue or heroism to reject the sin of greed universally—but it takes virtue to love one's own greedy boss. It was C. S. Lewis who made a wonderful discovery when he reflected on these truths. He realized that in one instance only was it easy to reject the reality of sin and to love the sinner: "For a long time I used to think this is a silly, straw-splitting distinction: how could you hate what a man did and not hate the man? But years later it occurred to me that there was one man to whom I had been doing this all my life—namely myself."[9]

Love Is Not Blind

One of the biggest misunderstandings about love is that it overlooks defects. Real love detects them and, if they are sinful, points them out so that they can be transformed. In the world of niceness, however, moral deficiencies are downplayed or rationalized. People say that someone committed a crime because he was a victim of this or that. Guilt has no place in the world of the nice god. It destroys the bubble we live in, demands that we take responsibility; and that is why guilt is under attack. Certainly, there are unhealthy forms of guilt—neuroses—but guilt as a moral compass should not be ignored.

It seems to me that there is a connection between the wrong understanding of love and the decline of guilt in our culture. If we just love enough, we can reduce the guilt people experience and make them happy again. That seems to be the conviction of many theologians, politicians, and entertainers. But this view rests on the assumption that love can diminish or wipe out objective guilt. It can absolve the pornography addict without confession or the adulterer without his having to feel guilty for his wrongdoing.

When people think and act this way, they *abuse* love and do the guilty person no favor. Because the nice god tells them, "It's all okay. Don't feel guilty. Just love!" they do not experience forgiveness, because they do not repent. They are drugged and brainwashed: They are told their guilt should not be there. They are told that moral deficiencies are normal and we should not take them so seriously.

God Takes Sin Seriously

Two modern atheists are responsible for this train of thought: first, Nietzsche, who claimed that Jews had invented guilt to ensure their survival; and second, Freud, who claimed that Jesus transformed human aggression into guilt complexes from which we have to free ourselves. Many theologians have followed these two, most of them unconscious of the origin of their nice theology that *seems* to take the human person so seriously.

Such theology downplays sin and gives up the ideal that each and every one of us should become a saint. One of the consequences of this nice theology is that the confessionals in Catholic churches are empty. Even parishes with a vibrant community often offer confession only once a week for half an hour. If a priest has three thousand parishioners and half an hour is sufficient to heal the wounded souls in his parish, he must minister only to saints.

The love of the real God, however, forgives rather than downplays sin. A good example is the adultery committed by King David (2 Sm 11:1–12:25): David cannot stop thinking about the wife of his general Uriah. He lusts for her. In order to get her into his bed and later on to hide her pregnancy, he sends her husband into war, where he dies on the battlefield. After the obligatory time of mourning, Bathsheba becomes David's wife.

A nice god would have minimized David's deed, but the God of Israel expresses his displeasure (2 Sm 12:11). He sends his prophet Nathan to ask the wise David his opinion of a story that Nathan tells to David. It is a slightly veiled tale that is actually all about David and his sins. David declares that the evildoer of the story deserves to die, and then realizes right after he has announced his verdict that he has effectively sentenced himself to death!

What follows is David's sincere repentance and plea for forgiveness. God indeed forgives him, but the child Bathsheba had conceived dies. To the reader this might suggest that God did not forgive David's sin or that he punishes the innocent of another generation for the sins of their fathers. The exegete Gerhard Lohfink, however, explains that such a reading would be theological nonsense. The text rather insinuates that every sin corrupts something in this world, even if the sin itself is forgiven.[10]

Imagine you start a rumor about your colleague in a Facebook post. Even if you feel truly sorry, apologize, and are forgiven by your colleague, you cannot take back the bad words you uttered—they have been disseminated through cyberspace into the minds of countless people. The effect of your sin will remain. Despite the fact that sins are forgiven, the shock waves they cause reverberate through the universe and can only be wiped out by the merits of our actions and the strength of our faith.

David's story therefore exemplifies that a loving God does not explain away the reality of sin but takes it seriously because he desires us to grow in faith, hope, and love. A nice god would not care for our transformation but would downplay the seriousness of our moral failures—all, of course, under the pretext of love. Real love never minimizes our responsibility but seriously assesses it: It is like a giant flashlight that shines painfully on our souls' diseases so that we can be healed. This light of God's love is so bright that if we accept it, it permeates even the darkest corners of our lives and makes them as radiant as the stars.

THE GOD OF INTIMACY

I ntimacy is usually associated with sex, but it has a much more intense meaning. The word has the Latin root *intimus*, which means "interior." It denotes a profound connection between humans. The word does not necessarily mean sex, but since sexual activity is usually such a profound exchange of mutually deep desires, we link it to that. Intimacy is, however, also present in friendships. In English we use the idiom "to be of kindred spirits" to express what intimacy is, because the sexual connotation of being intimate with somebody is too strong.

Being Naked

The great mystics of Christianity, especially women, have often spoken of their sensual love of God and describe the encounter with God as intimate. St. Teresa of Avila, Mechthild of Magdeburg, and others understood that being intimate with someone means to touch his or her innermost core and to be without masks in that very moment.

To be intimate with someone could therefore be defined as "being naked." Apart from its bedroom meaning, nakedness is, in the West, a taboo. One is only supposed to be naked for purposes of personal hygiene and in the sphere of one's private sexual activity. Nakedness in public is a clear no-no. Why? All humans need masks to protect themselves in a world that is out to exploit and to use people as things. Moreover, it is nonsensical that one can be friends with everyone. Not even social networks suggest this. Even in them, there are close circles of friends and wider circles of acquaintances. Shame protects and maintains the view that being naked is reserved for a handful of people who can be utterly trusted.

The Intimate God

If we look into the Old Testament, we find many examples in which the relationship with God is described like the intimate relationship with a lover. Let's look at a few. The book of Genesis narrates how God created humans. In the second creation account in Genesis, God breathes his spirit into a piece of clay that he has formed.

To share a breath with somebody is an act of intimacy; one shares the warm, humid air coming out of another person's mouth. That is why we take a step back when people do not respect our personal space or come too close to us in a conversation and share their breath with us against our will. The most common occasion when one shares another person's breath is, of course, during sexual intercourse, in moments of passion. Passion is an expression of liveliness, and liveliness is the opposite of niceness.[1]

God breathes life into Adam and makes him a partaker of divine life. Yet Adam feels alone and nothing can console him, so God forms Eve out of his rib. Sometimes people joke about this account as scientifically impossible. Well, yes, the Bible is not natural history but a story about more profound mysteries. Man and woman are intimately connected. They are not entirely different, but they are different enough. The story about the rib also confirms that women and men have the same dignity because they are in their very core identical human beings and partakers of God's care and life. The account tells us that God put Adam to sleep while he took his rib. God acts in this way not to deceive him or steal something from him but obviously to protect him from pain. The writer wants to show us that God is direct but also very gentle.

In numerous other instances, especially the account of Moses's exodus from Egypt and the Psalms, God is portrayed as one who can transform a "heart of stone" into a "heart of flesh." In other words, he can transform a sinner into a saint. Most readers of the Bible pass over such passages because they have encountered them so frequently and consequently miss that something very intimate is described here.

In order to work on somebody's heart, one has to open up the chest. Like a patient who undergoes open-heart surgery and has to patiently endure anesthetics and trust his surgeon, so is the human soul when God operates on it. The heart is also understood in the philosophical and poetic traditions of many cultures as the seat of the emotions. We talk about our "heavy heart" although we know that it is our brain and hormones that determine our feelings.

The Bible seems to insist that God values our emotions and interacts with them. Sometimes God is described as having feelings. While this is certainly a very human way of thinking about God, and imposes our limitations upon him, this ancient way of seeing God imparts an important insight that modern Christians have forgotten. It is that God's love for his people is not a benign nodding and patting on the back but something that cuts to our innermost core and is therefore described by the great mystics like a sexual experience.

The great theologian St. Augustine, who lived in the fourth century, has expressed this insight: God is "more intimate to me than I am to myself."[2] What could be more intimate? And in the garden of Eden, right after the creation and before the Fall, it is narrated that Adam and Eve walked with God through paradise. The point of this story is not that God likes to walk—this is again a very human way of thinking of God—but that they walked naked with God without being ashamed. Both were so close to God, were his closest friends, that they could be "naked" with him. We wear masks if we think we might get hurt, we hide if we are afraid, and we clothe ourselves for ordinary business. God's presence felt safe, and it was extraordinary. But once Adam and Eve sinned, the relationship changed. Suddenly both felt shame, covered their nakedness, and hid.

Covering Up Our Guilt

Psychoanalysts tell us that covering up guilt is a common way for people to deal with it—covering things up and hiding. It is interesting what happens next in the story of Adam and Eve. God looks for them and asks them what happened. If he is God, of course he knows that they ate from the forbidden tree, but he also knows that it is important to speak out loud about one's guilt. God knows the healing effect of being honest, intimate, with a friend.

This does not save the human couple from punishment, including expulsion from paradise, but before this happens, God gives Adam and Eve a present. Again, almost every commentary on the Bible overlooks this simple detail: God gives them new clothes made out of leather. When I teach my students about this story, I ask them where leather comes from. "From dead animals!" they realize. "And what does that mean?" I ask. God sacrifices one of his own creatures to give humans more permanent clothing and protection for their intimacy—he sheds blood to set things right, as the late Fulton Sheen has observed.[3]

It seems that while the relationship with God is broken on the human side—the "original wound" or "original sin"—God's love for humanity is untarnished. Just as the good father in Jesus' parable welcomes the prodigal son and has a valuable calf butchered, so too God slaughters an animal to clothe his human creatures—and we might add, to feed them with the flesh of the skinned animal. That God is portrayed as clothing and feeding his people demonstrates his desire to make clear that he is the core of our existence, without whom we are just stardust lost in a vast galaxy.

The Mystery of Forgiveness

But could God not have simply forgiven Adam and Eve? The Bible never doubts that he could have but tries to describe with stories that if he had done so, he would have destroyed something within humanity. Humans were created with freedom, and because of their free choice, evil came into the world.

If God had simply pardoned the first humans, they would not have learned their lesson—namely, that our actions have consequences. After all, they had been warned that if they ate from this tree they would die. They could have chosen any of the 999 other trees in the garden, but they didn't. If God had forgiven Adam and Eve, he would have been so nice—right? Actually, he would have been untruthful to them, not telling them that they broke his friendship and abused his trust. He would have been patting them on their heads, telling them not to do such things again. And Adam and Eve would have certainly reasoned that God can be easily manipulated because he does not keep his word. They would have stopped loving God, because how can one love somebody who does not keep his word and does not take one's moral development seriously?

The Bible, however, tells us that God punished Adam and Eve. And never once is it mentioned that they murmured about their punishment, because they knew it was just. It reminds me oddly of my own attempts at child education. One thing every parenting handbook considers the foundation of education is to be consistent. If I say that stealing a cookie from the cabinet means no dessert for a week, I have to stick with it or my child will never learn that actions have consequences and that Dad actually means what he says.

This brings us back to our concept of God as an intimate lover. Just as we love our children, so too God loves us, and therefore he cannot be a nice divine grandpa but instead the burning bush that sets our hearts on fire.

Without Masks

We began this chapter by explaining intimate love with the analogy of sexual love. Thus far we have not spoken much about sexual intercourse itself, which, strangely to some, expresses one of God's characteristics beautifully. I am here interested in why intercourse is used by the Bible and the Church as an analogy of God's love. When two partners love each other, they accept each other unconditionally. They say yes to each other's quirks and problems, trying to mend them or, if that's not possible, live with them. Real love extends beyond the worldly realm of what we can see.

When a couple has intercourse, both partners give themselves fully to each other in an act in which one forgets time and space. Good sex is an ecstatic experience—something that rips us out of our everyday routine—and therefore the Bible and the mystics compare this act with divine love. Loving God is not like loving a book or your garden or a piece of music. The God who is loving is gentle but passionate; he wants everything or nothing, like a lover.

No other book has expressed this facet of God's love more beautifully than the Song of Songs, a part of holy scripture contained in the Hebrew Bible that makes even the most experienced pastor blush when he has to preach about it. It is full of erotic, bridal love and sensuality. Like the lover who waits for his bride during the wedding night, so God waits for us. What passion! What sensuality! When we forget this passion and neglect our relationship with God, it becomes as dull as any other relationship we neglect. A husband who neglects his wife cannot expect a very fulfilling sex life with her.

It might be nice, but what is nice? A dull god might be content with a date; the biblical God is not.

Sexuality is also an image for the beauty that is God himself. The Greek philosopher Plato reminds us that every human person is determined to seek beauty and that one finds different grades of beauty. The highest degree of beauty is that which we enjoy by "vision." This does not mean the act of seeing something with our eyes but the enjoyment and contemplation of the object of beauty without being distracted. In the vision of beauty, one only thinks of beauty itself—and one of the best analogies to such an act is sex. When we love our partner, we think of nothing else but her.

Vulnerable Intimacy

Human sexuality also reminds us of another aspect of intimacy: we leave our clothes behind and are completely naked. In true intimacy, one does not wear masks but communicates oneself to another person. Franz Werfel, the great Jewish writer, once aptly observed that proper living means to "communicate oneself to others."[4] He was right, but we usually only do that with people whom we trust. We let our guard down and are figuratively naked only with those who will not judge us, mock us, or break our trust. We leave ourselves wide open to being hurt, and unfortunately but surely we sometimes will be hurt.

Christians believe that God has taken on human flesh in an act of perfect love. He made himself vulnerable, lowered himself to being a "slave," as the letter to the Philippians says (2:7). Most importantly, the Son did this to communicate to us the Father, as the first verses of the Gospel of John explain. We all know how this story ended: Jesus' trust is broken, his disciples desert him, and he is killed on the cross. Yet one aspect is always forgotten: Jesus' suffering. Why did Jesus die a violent death? He did so to save humanity from the consequences of sin and death. But could not God have just forgiven humanity?

He could decree a universal pardon for all sins for all time. Certainly. But I doubt he could *forgive*, because forgiveness always requires that the person is hurt first. A governor who pardons an inmate on death row is not the victim of the crime—he makes the decision at his desk. It is an act of clemency, but it has no moral value on the part of the governor because no virtue is needed to give or withhold the pardon.

If the parents, spouse, or children of the murdered victims forgive the murderer, then we can speak of a heroic act of forgiveness—a forgiveness that transcends their pain and their understandable desire for revenge. Forgiveness is an act similar to love and thus a deeply personal action.

When God decides to become vulnerable in the humanity of Christ, he arrives naked, as a baby. There is hardly anything more vulnerable than a child. In Bethlehem, he surrenders himself into the loving arms of a teenage girl named Mary and an elder foster father, Joseph. Only later does he become the object of violence: his opponents hate him, he is betrayed by Judas, he is painfully beaten, and he dies on the Cross by asphyxiation.

Scripture and the Church Fathers agree that Jesus *had* to suffer, yet the only explanation of why the Son of God would have to suffer is that he had to be personally affected by the effect of sin. He had to feel the hatred of humanity and the physical pain so that he could really forgive human sin once and forever. Only then does the excruciating death on the Cross, which historians call one of the most painful possible ways to die, make sense. Giving his life was an act of love, but the pains he endured were a necessary element of this love, because forgiveness presupposes being harmed. It is an openness, an intimacy of love that literally hurts. Such a God is not nice. In fact, calling him that would be a slap in his face.[5]

Love Is Procreative

A more positive aspect of intimate love is its creative side. Love that is unwilling to share is not love but selfishness. When two partners have sexual intercourse, they are open to receiving children, to sharing their joy with a new human being. Love creates new life!

A similar analogy of procreation is used by the English theologian and playwright Dorothy L. Sayers in *The Mind of the Maker*, namely, the creative mind of the writer. As a writer creates out of nothing a series of verses, so God creates the universe out of nothing. God does not start from a set of data to draw up a blueprint like an architect but shares his being, his existence, and that's why there is something rather than nothing. Creation is full of energy, full of life, and the opposite of boredom. The writer, however, also reminds us of how to handle the world: if we see the world as a series of problems that we have to master, we become rigid machines, Sayers argues. That is why I think Erich Fromm and Dorothy L. Sayers complement each other so beautifully: they start from different presuppositions but come to the same conclusion—that true love has to do with art and creation! Just as an artist has to abandon the idea of ever becoming the "best" artist, so we have to abandon the illusion of ever completely mastering our lives and instead cooperate with it in love, because a true artist knows that he will never be perfect.[6] There is no creatively solving problems because the act of creation is utterly different from analytic problem solving. Creation involves love and sacrifice: "The perfect work of love demands co-operation of the creature, responding according to the law of its nature," Sayers says.[7]

By creating something with our minds or hands, or especially by creating new life out of an act of love, humans participate in divine action. The latter is a central aspect of the Theology of the Body of St. John Paul II, who regarded the mutual yes of the spouses as the key to understanding God's yes to humanity.

Love can never be just nice, and it is therefore a complete misunderstanding of God and our own faith life if we think of him or of our commitment to him as such. Love is always intimate; it touches our core and is thus much more than an emotion. And the mystery of conjugal love that brings forth new life reminds us that human existence is not about problem solving but about cooperation with God's intentions.

THE GOD OF CONSOLATION

When I turn on the morning news, usually only after the first cup of coffee, I often think, *There is the proof of original sin.* It doesn't matter whether a mass shooting occurred or whether I have to watch the coverage of a vain celebrity; I gaze at the abyss of humanity and I don't exclude myself from the mess. After all, I am a fallen creature, too. Original sin affects all of us; not only are we wandering through a thicket of sin and temptation but we for sure are also no longer in paradise. Of course, you might answer, we all have to work and sweat and suffer—but I don't mean that either. I mean that we have lost the most important element of paradise—being in intimate friendship with the infinite God.

The Gaping Hole in Our Souls

Ever since our friendship with God was broken, our souls have been wounded. We suffer from the expulsion not from an earthly paradise where we do not work or feel pain but from the fulfillment of our infinite desire. In paradise, the desire was met through our friendship with the infinite God. What is this infinite desire in us? It is there.

I have felt it. I have seen others suffering from it, and it seems all humans have it—we are never content.

We think some earthly good might make us happy. We pursue these supposedly good things only to realize that we want a bigger and better version of them—and do not see that this chasing after earthly goods (or often spiritual ones, too) is a symptom of the original wound we bear. One of my favorite examples is a good dinner. When we have a dinner party, the conversation tends to shift at some point to food; suddenly, while we are enjoying a wonderful meal, we are discussing recipes and what we might cook next time. We are already planning the next great thing! Or we believe that we will be happier after the next promotion, after the next raise, and so forth. It is an illusion that St. Augustine long ago saw through. The gaping hole in our souls, brought about by original sin, is a vacuum, a bottomless pit that only the infinite can fill. It is like the Grand Canyon, and we think we can fill it by throwing a few pebbles into it! An infinite need demands an infinite fulfillment, logic tells us.

The truth is, what we long for is the mystery of God. Why do I say all this? What does it have to do with our concept of God? If we start out with a weak concept of god, or a nice god, we set ourselves up for failure. In the back of our minds, we believe that the tame, boring god cannot fulfill us or meet our infinite desires. And because of this usually unconscious belief, we dare not expose ourselves to this god in all our vulnerability. We do not want to be naked in front of this god. All we desire then is a short-lived pleasant experience, some numbness from pain but not that the hole in our heart be closed. We want a bandage, but God offers open-heart surgery.

Many Christians today have turned God into a pleasant, kind deity. He is no longer a mystery but a finite idol. However, as Karl Pfleger, a German-French theologian, reminds us, "Only the Mystery can console us."[1] A god who is constructed by us and who only watches over our earthly needs, like a glorified Santa, is not able to console us and fulfill the heart's true desire, because he is no longer infinite and incomprehensible. More importantly, he is too mundane and too similar to earthly life.

The novelist François Mauriac, who won the Nobel Prize for Literature, was once asked if he painted human life in such dark colors because he hated the world. He rejected that notion. All he wanted, he insisted, was to portray life as it is, as dark and cruel with hints of joy and brightness mixed therein. By doing so, he only highlighted the beauty and complete otherworldliness of God, which we so often forget. Only when we take the world with all its suffering seriously do we realize that God alone can save it and what a tragedy it would be to sacrifice our lives to the monster of worldliness. Only then do we realize how utterly different God is from this world.

Diversion Is a Drug

Many no longer see such suffering because they have been brainwashed by advertisements that health, retirement savings, global warming, education of one's children and grandchildren, the economy, and rising interest rates are the truly important things in life. Of course, marketing specialists never say these goods are the most important ones. They create all kinds of different "needs," each of which we supposedly have to fulfill in order to be happy. They create diversion. They do not want us to realize that the most important things in life cannot be bought and are gifted to us!

This diversion agenda is nothing new and has probably existed from the beginning of humanity, or rather from the beginning of *sinful* humanity. Long ago, Blaise Pascal, the great seventeenth-century mathematician and philosopher, warned about this:

> From childhood on men are burdened . . . with duties
> . . . and given to understand that they can never be happy
> unless their health, honor, their fortune, and those of
> their friends are in good shape, and that it needs only

> one thing to go wrong to make them unhappy. So they are given responsibilities and duties which harass them from the first moment of each day. . . . You would only have to take away all their cares, and then they would see themselves and think about what they are, where they come from and where they are going.[2]

In a busy life, there is no space for asking the big questions, and there is no place left for expressing the infinite longing for the mystery of existence.

Today the situation is perhaps even worse, as diversion has become not just a commodity but a universal drug. We are no longer individuals but members of a mass society, whose needs are dictated by large companies. We live under the delusion that we are free but do not see that our choices are created by businesses that want us to buy their products. Constantly we receive exclusive membership deals; we are members of the savers' club at our grocery store, members of the book club, friends with many others on Facebook, with lots of followers on Twitter. Yet rarely, if ever, do we think of ourselves as members of the Body of Christ—not of the Church and not of our parish but of the blood-drenched, wounded, suffering, yet glorious body of the Lord. The more we are numbed by diversion, the more we become deaf to the individual suffering and pain around us.

Keep the Pain Away

Humanitarians raise awareness of groups that are in need or collect finances to address suffering as an abstract reality. We give money to good abstract causes and exculpate ourselves. We have done our duty and at the same time are assured that individual suffering stays out of our sight. The consequence is that we have now begun to see all kinds of evils as abstract realities we can delegate to some organization to solve. The suffering of our neighbors has become something we deal with and no longer a crisis that touches us. That, of course, changes when our own existence is suddenly threatened and when suffering grabs us. Then, we readjust our expectations in life: if our child has cancer, it no longer matters what car we drive or whether the roof leaks a bit.

The point I am trying to make is that the God Christians pray to has always been one we believe can alleviate our suffering, either through his intervention—be it in a miracle or through people he sends our way—or by consoling us. And in the end, God assures us that things will be set right—namely, that the evildoers will be punished and their victims avenged.

A god who is a kind, Santa-like deity that is responsible for our health, our house, and our finances is hardly the God who would permit pain and interrupt our lives. C. S. Lewis, the great apologist for the Christian faith, therefore called pain God's "megaphone" and was heavily criticized for it. He did not mean that God creates pain and suffering, but he believed—in accord with the entire Christian tradition—that God permits evil and uses it for his own (good) ends. God can bring about good from evil.

One of the best arguments against the existence of such a benevolent god is that God could have prevented all evil from the very beginning. Yet we have seen that there is no freedom of the will if we cannot also abuse it. If we were to suffer endlessly, such a life would indeed pose a challenge to the belief in God; but all our earthly suffering has an end since we are finite. Our death not only robs us of the beauty of life but also frees us from suffering. In this sense, there is also no *unlimited* suffering because it is always one human being or one animal that suffers—there is no such thing as the pain of a people or the pain of an animal species.

In the end, it is always individuals who suffer, and God has wisely limited that suffering through individual death. The suffering of the damned in hell does not contradict this plan because, as Lewis put it in *The Great Divorce*, their pain is self-inflicted: by rejecting God, they reject reality and impose pain on themselves.[3] A mole cannot survive on the earth's surface because he lacks eyesight; the beams of the sun hurt him. Likewise, the damned do not want to see God but are in his radiant light, which hurts them but gives endless joy to those with eyes of faith and love.

The God Who Sets Things Right

Pain is a reality in all our lives—the question is how we deal with it. If we do not believe in the mysterious God who is the reason for all existence, we have nobody who can console us in our pain and, worse, no one who can set things right. The philosopher Immanuel Kant called this his "moral argument for the existence of God." All our moral actions would be in vain if there was no God because, as we experience daily, it is not advantageous to be virtuous but rather to be immoral. If there is no institution or person that after this earthly life rewards those who have struggled for a moral life and punishes those who have been immoral, then a virtuous life makes no sense.

Kant, himself a deeply virtuous person, drew the conclusion that we must assume the existence of God if we do not want our animal drives to take over and we do not want to become egomaniacal monsters. Atheist philosophers indeed have trouble giving reasons for why people should be moral, because all moral laws are for them merely societal conventions (which can change!) and never eternal laws. There cannot be any objective moral truth in an atheist philosophy.

Most famously, Bertrand Russell tried to reconcile his own activism for the peace movement with the realization that his actions were not morally good because according to his philosophy there was no such thing. Russell embodied what the Catholic philosopher Jacques Maritain called a "disinterested" positive atheist—a person who is willing to give himself totally to the world and is "satisfied to die in it, as a blade of grass in the loam, and to make it more fertile

by dissolving in it. . . . The positive atheist delivers over his own soul
. . . to a worldly demiurge."[4] This demiurge is an idol, what Auguste
Comte meant when he spoke of "belief in Humanity."[5]

It is important to stress what I am *not* saying. I am not saying that atheists are immoral, far from it. Rather, I argue that their
conviction is inconsistent: there is no absolute moral standard that
would make their sacrifices of life or their moral stances rational,
because without the existence of God there are no absolute, objective moral truths. Russell stated in his famous book *Why I Am Not
a Christian* his belief that:

> Man is the product of causes which had no prevision of
> the end they were achieving; that his origin, his growth,
> his hopes and fears, his love and beliefs, are but the out-
> comes of accidental collocations of atoms; that no fire,
> no heroism, no intensity of thought and feeling, can pre-
> serve individual life beyond the grave; that all the labors
> of the ages, all the devotion, all the noonday brightness
> of human genius, are destined to extinction in the vast
> death of the solar system, and that the whole temple of
> Man's achievement must inevitably be buried beneath
> the debris of a universe in ruins. . . . Only within the
> scaffolding of these truths, only on the firm foundation
> of unyielding despair, can the soul's habitation henceforth
> be safely built.[6]

Why Did Jesus Have to Suffer?

In the end, the heroic belief in humanity that Comte and Russell
proposed is built on the insight of despair—that there is no hope,
no consolation. I will go so far as to say that for a person who only
believes in the kind, deist god, there can be hardly more than despair,
too. A limited god would be powerless in the face of evil. He might
try to persuade others to love, as the so-called school of process

philosophy maintains, but he could not eliminate suffering and evil or set things right at the end of time. Any limitation on God's attributes—be they omnipresence, omnipotence, omniscience, justice, benevolence, etc.—creates a finite being that is no longer God. Certainly, such a being is more comprehensible because it would be more similar to a human being, but it would not be able to console our pain, direct all evil to a good end, or set things right.

Believing that God is the one who sets things right gives us a new understanding of the suffering of Jesus. For centuries, the standard explanation of his sacrifice on the cross has been that of St. Anselm, an eleventh-century theologian—namely, that Christ made satisfaction for the sins of the world. Anselm's doctrine seems to leave out one key aspect: Jesus' *extensive suffering* during his Passion and Crucifixion. According to Anselm, death itself is the act of satisfaction.

A German Catholic philosopher, Fr. Harald Schöndorf, S.J., has built upon Anselm's thinking and suggested a new way of looking at the suffering Jesus. He sees the key to unlocking the mystery in the Our Father request, "Forgive us our trespasses, as we forgive those who trespass against us." There seems to be an inherent connection between the forgiveness of God and our forgiveness of sins committed against us. Yet in order to understand forgiveness, we have to clarify sin. Sin means committing an act against God, which brings as an automatic consequence, if done with full knowledge of the grave nature of the act and with full consent of one's will, death and destruction for the sinner and those affected by the sin. We have to differentiate this from venial sin, which damages our friendship with God but does not destroy it. Both violate the just order God has created.

Ever since Plato, philosophers have argued that the punishment of the evildoer restores this justice. Yet the restoration is never complete. One only has to think of an ugly divorce, where the hurt and the hostility remain even after a settlement. Real justice would include the elimination of all bad effects of the evil deed—something we can never achieve.

Nevertheless, reconciliation is able to bring about precisely that through repentance and forgiveness. Therefore, God's mercy and forgiveness are the higher form of justice! Are there any presuppositions for forgiveness? For Schöndorf, it is the suffering of Christ Jesus. Only if God is deeply affected by our sins can he enter the process of reconciliation and forgiveness; otherwise, he would simply pardon us. When Jesus is exposed to terrible contempt and torture and finally condemned to death, God becomes the object of humanity's hatred and sin in a personalized way that cannot be superseded. After the Passion and Death of Jesus, God could truly forgive and restore justice. Therefore, Jesus "had to suffer" (Lk 24:26, ISV) so that he could forgive us in a convincing, persuasive way: by looking at the crucifix, we believe that God suffered and therefore was truly affected by our wrongdoing.[7]

The Choice Is Ours

In the end, we face a crossroads: either we go with Bertrand Russell's philosophy of despair and atheism or we side with the traditional Christian answer to it—that there is a God who cares for our suffering, even shares in it.

There is no middle ground. A weak God could possibly care but not act on our behalf and not ensure our eternal life. Only the God of thunder, terror, surrender, and intimacy—as we described the God of Abraham, Isaac, and Jacob, and the Father of Jesus Christ in the previous chapters—can do that. Nevertheless, it is an act of faith to surrender ourselves into his arms. The philosopher Peter Wust, who died in 1940 after a long struggle with cancer, wrote that in the midst of insecurity about our own existence and eternal life, we are contained in the love of God, in the half-shadow of the divine that will only be lifted once we enter into his realm.[8]

THE GOD OF INCARNATION

Christianity is so perfectly scandalous because it does not leave God on the mantel or in the temple but actually claims that he entered our world. Indeed, it is not even content with that: he was born like us, grew up like us, worked like us, and died like us. This mystery of the Incarnation, of the enfleshment of the Son of God, who was resurrected from the dead, is a thorn in our desire to control our private space. This Christian God is indeed like a robber in the night (Mt 24:43), disturbing our sleep and invading our home. Jesus, who uses this image, is therefore not at all nice!

Don't Focus on Feelings

Nice people give us pleasure, or at least contentment. We like listening to their jokes, we feel entertained by their singing or their company, but we do not seek them in moments of pain. Why? Because we intuitively know that we do not expect them to share our feelings, to be compassionate in our misery, or to listen sincerely. A nice person would say "Everything will be well" or "It's not all bad" but would not sit with us in the ruins of our life in silence and share our despair.

We know this, however, only because we decided beforehand to see the nice person not as a human being but as a persona, a mask for pleasant conversations only. Niceness is a *sentimentalist virtue*. It is an artificial feeling of happiness. Everything that can cause a negative feeling is banned. Yet sentimentalism is only a state of mind and as such is inferior to action, which always has an intended object or agenda.

And therein the problem really lies. If I am a sentimentalist, I obsessively focus on having the right feeling and thus suffocate my personal growth—I remain on the narcissist level of a two-year-old, who thinks the world exists only to fulfill my wishes.[1] Nonsentimentalists, that is, people who have maintained a sense for real-life values, have an intuitive awareness of such sentimentalist shallowness; therefore, they only share their experience of pain with those who are capable of listening.

Does God Want Us to Be Happy?

It is telling of our society that we have even turned God into a sentimentalist. In fact, many of our children learn from the first hour of Sunday school that God wants everybody to be happy. Some parents might object that a different image of God would terrify their children. I don't think so—and I am speaking with the experience of parenting five kids. Children have a natural sense of justice and of true joy. They understand that it would be bad if everybody was granted happiness in her own right, so that everyone can enjoy herself. God intends the best for us—ultimate happiness—but that does not mean painlessness on earth. Yet it is exactly this, that many believe about God's plans for us. C. S. Lewis has summed it up like this: "We want in fact, not so much a Father in heaven as grandfather in heaven—a senile benevolence," who lets us have a good time.[2]

Such a God could exist. He would leave us be, because he would not care much for us. What?—some will object. Would such a God truly respect our freedom and our needs? He would not. A parent who lets his children do what they want and shelters them from every unhappy feeling just raises monsters. I would rather have my children experience suffering if that is for their best than constant kindness that suffocates their souls.

The same applies to God, who loves us and seeks to bring about our transformation. St. Paul compares this process to the excruciating pains of childbirth (Rom 8:18–23). It is for an increasing number of contemporaries unfathomable that God would allow (not create!) pain to bring about a greater good. Instead, some churches have created the kind grandfather-god Lewis feared, who is like a mall greeter worthy of a smile but not of us sharing our life with him. Such a god is shut out from our emotional realm, unworthy of a personal dialogue, which we call prayer.

In fact, for many today, prayer is intended to make oneself "feel better" and to get worries off one's chest. There is nothing wrong with asking God for certain things, and it is good to bring worries and fears to him; it all depends on how we do it. If we pray because we feel some consolation and we want this feeling of consolation, we do not seek God but, again, an emotion. We make God part of our wellness, and that is, strictly speaking, an abuse of God. Every great mystic knew that prayer is not about us but about the divine, and that consolation is a gift that vanishes quickly when one enters the higher stages of communication with God. It is a temptation to remain at a lower stage just because it feels better and because we are afraid of the spiritual wasteland—the dark night of the soul, as St. John of the Cross called it—that comes next.

But these drier episodes of prayer life can also be an important lesson, teaching us to focus on God and how God wants us to grow in trust. They can show us how God wants to guide our will rather than our curiosity or intellect by images and thoughts. For sure, this is not nice of God. St. Thérèse of Lisieux suffered tremendously under the sudden hiddenness of God in her prayer life even though she promised to do everything in her life out of love for Christ. St. Teresa of Calcutta had a very similar experience.[3]

Why would God allow the feeling of his absence? The human nature of Jesus himself also experienced this on the cross. And why? For our sake: because it is important for us to learn that we should love God for *who he is* and not for *what he does for us*. How empty would a relationship be if we loved our spouse only for the good feelings he or she stirs in us? The same applies to the divine, of course. Only a relationship that is honest can grow into sincere love. Only a real God interested in our eternal welfare would act like this, rather than with niceness.

No God for Marginal Things

We create another extreme form of the wellness-god by eliminating prayer and communication with him about the truly important questions in life. This god is left only with our peripheral wellness and worries: "Please let me get that annual bonus!" or "Let me get a raise!" and the like. Prayers such as "Guide my way to truth and let me find Jesus every day better and better" are not on the horizon of such a person.

Unconsciously, many who pray only about the small things in life, such as economic prosperity, health, or the safety of their house, no longer actually trust God with the big things. They have made their plans for their life and have ideas of how it should develop. God as a true guide, and the Holy Spirit as a whispering, even interfering influence, are not welcome. God has become unworthy of profound dialogue.

The idea of distancing God from real personal communication—the kind that we have with only our best friends and family—goes back to the 1700s. At that time, a number of theologians worked on reforming theology and bringing it into dialogue with modern science and thought. The constancy of natural laws struck them as especially awe-inspiring. Yet it led them to believe that if God had designed the universe with these (allegedly) eternal laws, then it would be below his majesty to deal with the marginal things of the universe, like the prayers of an English peasant. A God who listened to prayers and answered them seemed to these deists like a superhuman in heaven and thus as irrational.

What the deists did not realize, however, was that they modeled their new image of the gracious, majestic lawgiver—who leans back on his throne and does not bother with the minuscule facets of creation—on their conception of majesty embodied in the French and English monarchies. Thus, the biblical God was replaced with a superhuman absolutist king. Such a god could not be bothered with guiding our lives. Like a welfare provider, however, he could be asked for special favors.

Although most churches rejected the most radical forms of this view, it nevertheless made it into the theology books of the time. One could not think of a better way of explaining that God ruled the world through his providence but seldom intervened. The concept of the "general will" of God was born, which reigned through eternal laws, while his "special will" was aimed at specific events in world history. This was a calamitous development as it rendered almost everything unimportant, especially the areas of life in which people need God the most: during pain and suffering.

Once cut off from the ear of God, people searched for replacements for their lost companion and different solutions for dealing with their pain. In the twentieth century, many turned to psychotherapy and most recently to health fanaticism. Because we are unable to face the ultimate pain of our life and the reality of our death, and to look suffering in the eye, we have come to believe that a painless existence, a healthy life, is the highest good on earth. This health activism has developed into a new religion with its own

dogmas, rituals, and priests. Doctors and fitness trainers have taken
the role of pastors and are often seen as compassionate life coaches.

This is all the more questionable if one remembers that health
is defined as a state free from illness and pain. Yet how can a painless existence—which is, according to the research of the German
psychiatrist Manfred Lütz, not more than 9.82 percent of our life
span—be the highest good?[4]

Health is important, but no major thinker in the history of
humankind has ever seen it as the highest good—until now. Why?
No generation has been so afraid of pain and death as ours. So many
believe there is nobody "out there" with whom they can share their
fears and who understands them. Taylor Caldwell wrote a beautiful
novel called *The Listener* about this modern experienc. She is certain
that a person's "real need, his most terrible need, is for someone to
listen to him, not as a 'patient,' but as a human soul. He needs to
tell someone of what he thinks, of the bewilderment he encounters
when he tries to discover why he was born, how he must live, and
where his destiny lies. The questions he asks of psychiatrists are not
the questions in his heart, and the answers he receives are not the
answers he needs."[5]

Yet instead of facing this fear or looking for a remedy—as
the medieval Christians did when they led the rich to coffins with
decomposing corpses to confront them with the finitude of their
importance or decorated churches with smiling human skeletons—
we have decided to deny the reality of pain and death. We choose
the nice life instead of the religious life that offers to heal the whole
person, overcome death, and transform earthly existence into everlasting bliss.

Quality of Life Includes Choice

What determines our quality of life? I would say, first of all, the love
of people around me, access to clean water and food, and the ability

to do the essential things I like doing. If health were really the highest good, our governments would have to spend much more on health care—in fact, they would have to spend themselves to bankruptcy. Can I have a high quality of life even if I have a heart defect and cannot run a marathon or if I have a peanut allergy and cannot enjoy them? Of course! Yet with such limitations I am not healthy by the common understanding of most people, not completely, at least. However, nobody is completely healthy. We have certain standards according to which our cholesterol level might be fine, our blood pressure is acceptable, and so on, but look a bit further and you might find a slight aberration here and there. This is so because health is not the complete absence of defects but rather the absence of defects and illnesses that *impede* me from doing what I want to be doing.

This brings us to the problem that in order to be healthy, we have to *choose to be so*. Of course, we cannot just decide to be cancer-free, but we can decide to make the best out of the situation and enjoy our life. Especially if we believe that our earthly existence is only a temporary pilgrimage, we should not be overly concerned with the length of our existence. But it is here where the religion of health tries to back us into a corner.

The new dogma is simple: One has to live as long as possible. One has to be fit to avoid illnesses that shorten one's life. I do not think we should be reckless with our health; all religions teach that one is obliged to reasonably care for one's body, and Christians even believe it to be the temple of the Holy Spirit because Jesus Christ himself took on human flesh. But the good of the body is not the ultimate good. Conduct an experiment. Tell someone that you have no intention of living up to ninety years of age but that you would rather enjoy your life—not by wrecking your body but by doing what you like. You will probably earn a frown. Death has to be avoided—how could somebody embrace death? Fitness, raw vegetables, and regular enemas will prolong the inevitable, make us live longer, with the possibility that a cure for death might eventually be found. Of course, most do not say this explicitly, but it is perhaps being asserted if we read between the lines. The nice religion of health cannot face the ultimate reality, however. It never can. Only the God who experienced death and overcame it can do that.

The real tragedy is that it was so easy for the religion of health to replace God. He was already relegated to a mantelpiece long ago and is only taken down on Sundays. In other words, for at least the last two hundred years, Christians have increasingly ignored the aspects of their religion that talk about a God who heals. Consequently, fewer and fewer people opened up their hearts to him and showed their wounds, and because they did not expose their pain, they could not be healed.

When I prepare second-graders for their first confession, I tell them a story: Imagine you go to the doctor, moaning with pain, but every time the doctor asks you "Where does it hurt?" or "What is the nature of your discomfort?" you fall silent. It will be almost impossible even for the greatest diagnostician to identify your condition. That is why we utter it in words in the sacrament of Penance, so that Christ can heal us from the wounds our sins have caused.

None other than the father of modern psychotherapy, Sigmund Freud, realized in the 1930s the healing power of verbalizing traumas, dreams, and past experiences of all sorts. But since healing is expected from the doctor, the therapist, the fitness trainer, and the chiropractor, God has become the receiver of moral checklists. "I have committed adultery. Please forgive me. Check." "I have spread rumors. Please forgive me. Check." Many people who call themselves religious see God only as the authority to forgive their moral trespasses. Their slate should be wiped clean, but as for healing, they no longer expect it. God is today so completely disconnected from the everyday experience of healing that he has been replaced by the elliptical trainer, Prozac, and bran flakes.

The Mental Teddy Bear God

The same people who fall asleep during a sermon have no problem reading three hundred pages about how fiber and vitamins will save them from an early death. Yet one cannot joke with the followers of health religion. This nice new religion has no humor: I once joked that because a friend had decided to run a mile every day, he would certainly live one week longer than me. While I laughed, my friend looked furious because I had just ridiculed his belief that health and a long life were the greatest values.

All major monotheistic religions, be it Judaism, Christianity, or Islam, teach that health is a good for which one should be grateful but also that the highest good is union with God in heaven. None of the great philosophers, be it Plato, Aristotle, Aquinas, Kant, or Nietzsche, would have called a fragile good such as health the highest good of all. Yet frequently at parties and other social occasions, I hear, "I wish you health. That is the most important thing in life." Is it?

Fanatics of the health religion decide to ignore the ubiquitous human fear of death at their peril. They are feeding on the illusion that life can be indefinitely prolonged. Again, none of them would openly confess that they believe this, but if they were honest with themselves, they would realize the vanity of calling health the highest good. The German philosopher Odo Marquard called the ideology of a perfect earthly life "the mental teddy bear" of modern childish adults.[6]

When God Became an Atheist

The God of Incarnation also is not nice since he did not even spare his own Son from the pains of human existence. (Not to mention the fact that that Son lived a short life of only thirty-some years!) From the earliest days of Christianity, there was the conviction that the pain Jesus endured was not a masquerade but real and that a person of the Holy Trinity had suffered.

This does not mean, however, that the eternal God suffered, but only that the divine person united with the human body of Jesus Christ suffered. This all sounds very complicated and it would be much easier to say that God suffered, as some twentieth-century theologians claim. This solution, however, runs into a major problem: If God suffers pain, how can he still be the guarantor of overcoming pain? In other words, how can the sick person be the healer and healed himself?

Therefore, most theologians realized that the ancient formulation was wisely chosen as it hints at the mystery that only the human nature of Christ suffered. It is worthwhile to spend some time on this, because we usually think only of the Crucifixion of Jesus as his suffering. This might make it harder for many to identify with him, because they cannot see any similarity with their own pain. But a closer look at the life of Jesus reveals more.

If we read the gospels, we encounter a man used to suffering. First-century Palestine was not a comfortable place to grow up, so we can rightly assume he endured childhood sicknesses, some of which might have looked to Mary as if they threatened his life. Early on, he experienced the loss of his earthly foster father, Joseph. We do not know how old he was at that time, but Jesus must have been a teenager or in his twenties, as Joseph had brought his son to the Temple at age twelve (Lk 2:41–52).

As every parent of a teenager knows, to lose somebody that close in the formative phase of adolescence is a deep incision. The biblical text does not enlighten us as to what Jesus felt, but he must have experienced a loneliness similar to what he endured twenty years later in the garden of Gethsemane.

It is likely that Jesus had nephews, nieces, and more cousins than just John the Baptist. At that time, there was a high infant mortality rate, so nothing speaks against the possibility of the boy Jesus mourning the loss of other relatives as well.

Finally, during his ministry, he experienced not only the betrayal of two of his closest friends, Judas and Peter, but also the desolation and desertion of his other disciples. The Gospel of Mark (14:51–52) illustrates this beautifully: one disciple, stopped by the Temple guards, jumps out of his clothes and runs away naked—and thus in a state of utter shame—to avoid being arrested with Jesus.

Yet the ultimate moment of suffering is a different one. It is not the crown of thorns, the nailing to the Cross, or the slow asphyxiation, as painful as these were. Jesus' cry on the Cross, "My God, my God, why have you forsaken me?" (Mt 27:46), is the expression of utter loneliness in the moment of death—a fear every human person has, because ultimately everybody dies alone, regardless of how many friends accompany the process of dying. By throwing the human nature of Jesus into the abyss of this darkness, it seems as if God for a moment became an atheist himself, or as G. K. Chesterton put it:

> When the world shook and the sun was wiped out of heaven, it was not at the crucifixion, but at the cry from the cross: the cry which confessed that God was forsaken of God. And now let the revolutionist choose a creed from all the creeds and a god from all the gods of the world, carefully weighing all the gods of the inevitable recurrence and of unalterable power. They will not find another god who has himself been in revolt. Nay . . . but let the atheists themselves choose a god, they will find only one divinity who ever uttered their isolation; only one religion in which God seemed for an instant to be an atheist.[7]

Jesus' cry on the Cross should therefore be understood as the ultimate proof that God wants to listen to our fears, relieve our anger, and transform our pain into something beautiful, as the Resurrection shows. The fact that even God Incarnate felt forsaken should remind each of us that the Christian God is everything but nice: he has time to listen with compassion because he has suffered it all.

The God Who Answers Our Prayers

But even if we believe that God listens, does God act on behalf of our prayers? Have we ever really experienced that a prayer was answered just as we had wished for? Sometimes, perhaps. Many times, though, we feel as if God is not answering. Each person who struggles to maintain a life of prayer can relate to this experience. In fact, many great saints, such as St. Teresa of Calcutta, did not feel any personal consolation in their prayers but kept on praying because God was answering their prayers in different and unexpected ways.

If God was nice, he would indeed respond to my prayers as I send them up to him. But would that be preferable? Often I pray selfishly and forget what is truly important in life. I pray to complete a research project, for a much-needed salary increase, or to be spared from the stomach flu my youngest child has brought home. If every prayer was answered, I fear I would become a supernarcissist.

In those moments, it is good to remind oneself that the Latin translation of the Bible, the Vulgate, makes clear that the request "give us our daily bread" in the Our Father means the bread of the Eucharist and not our earthly goods. The original Greek of the New Testament uses the unique word *epi-ousion* to demonstrate this. It means something like "supersubstantial"—that which is beyond our earthly being. If we reflect on this request for a moment, it becomes clear why it mirrors our prayerful existence: we ask God for something material we need—and we might need it badly—but forget the supernatural reality we should be concerned with. Like a parent, Jesus is instructing us how to pray and how to put first things first, and second things second. Give us this day our supersubstantial bread—make us worthy to receive the bread that gives eternal life.[8]

Is Our Faith Worth Dying For?

Considering the above, it would follow that a nice God cannot embrace pain and that nice people can't either. This should serve as a wake-up call for us. Is the religion we are living worth dying for?

Hopefully none of us has to face the option of choosing between faith and life, and, of course, we think of ancient and contemporary martyrs, but ultimately we face this question: Is this faith worth shaping my entire life? Or, put differently, is it worth sacrificing everything I hold dear in this world?

I always tell my students, "If your faith is not worth sacrifices, find a nice hobby and don't waste your time going to church." First, the students are shocked to hear this statement from a theology professor, but once the words have sunk in, they realize what I mean: if one is not committed to a religion, it is a worthless, ugly ornament.

In the history of Christianity we can find countless martyrs—people who gave their lives for their creed. Sociologists confirm that martyrs are the most credible exponents of the value of a religion, and outsiders to religion often wonder what could have motivated them to renounce their lives rather than their belief. It seems counterintuitive that people follow a religion that demands high costs or the highest sacrifice of all: one's life.

An economist would tell us that, other things remaining equal, a group that imposes high costs on its members, be it social stigmas or persecution or other forms of sacrifice, is less attractive. The interesting thing with religion, however, is that things do not remain equal. The higher the costs of membership, the stronger the levels of commitment.

Sociologist Rodney Stark explains that two things are responsible for this outcome. First, by demanding sacrifices, a religion eliminates free riders—those who try to sneak in to receive the benefits but are not fully committed. Second, the sacrifices increase participation of the members because the payoff for involvement has increased. Therefore, it runs against sociological logic to decrease demands on church members in order to be all-inclusive and to pretend that the purpose of our faith is a series of touchy-feely wellness events.[9]

The God of Abraham, Isaac, and Jacob is not nice when he asks his followers to fulfill his covenant by sacrificing their lives. This includes living according to his moral expectations, but first of all it requires putting God first, not just on Sundays but every minute of the day. This requirement runs against our human nature and our societal training to be autonomous, to think of ourselves, and to view God as one who lets us do whatever we want and only demands a few prayers once a week.

A nice god would not be worth our attention. He could not take us seriously because he would want to escape pain, and as an all-powerful being he would do so successfully. A nice god would by definition have no interest in our sufferings, or in our deepest joys. He would be like milk toast. Many people live with such a demon and think it is god. It is much easier to have a weak demon-god in one's life who does not ask too much of us, but in the moment of heartbreaking suffering, the idol will be shattered. Then one crawls back to the burning bush with the real God, at least until one feels better. Either the real God or none—time is too valuable for anything else.

THE GOD OF REBIRTH

Large segments of society seem to have forgotten what sin means. For them, there is no objective evil anymore, and they have stopped believing that sin destroys our friendship with God. Even churchgoing Christians have learned to reject the traditional meaning of sin and of original sin. I heard one parishioner say recently after a baptism, "Well, in my eyes that baby has done nothing wrong. I can't see any original sin in a newborn."

There are at least two things wrong with such a statement. First, you cannot ever see sin, either in a baby or in an adult. That is why we should never judge the state of grace of others: we do not truly know whether someone has committed a mortal sin unless we have seen it, and even then we might not know if that person went to confession afterward or was fully culpable. Second and more important is the fact that this is a complete misunderstanding of original sin. And if we get original sin wrong, we also get God, Christ, salvation, and the Church wrong, so a clarification seems more than justified.

What Original Sin Is and Isn't

Many who reject original sin or announce they have "problems" with it seem to think that God gave an unreasonable command— namely, not to eat from a particular tree although he knew that humans would be unable to keep this command. Consequently, the punishment of Adam and Eve seems unfair in their eyes, and a God whose Church upholds original sin as dogma appears to be vengeful at worst and a bean counter at best.

Original sin is a dogma for every Catholic, and to dismiss it as an unfortunate invention of St. Augustine, as some do, is utterly false. Relying on tradition, Augustine articulated what original sin was in such a sophisticated way that the Church accepted his wording as the best possible way of framing the truth.

Original sin is not just about the disobedience of Adam and Eve. It is, in its core, primarily about the relationship of humans with God—the fact that we are born not into a community of holiness but into a broken world. Nobody is born a Catholic—nobody! We become members of the Church by baptism. It is also about the worldly condition of humanity and the "chasm of this condition with the image of perfection and happiness that the human person carries in her soul."[1] We carry an image of hope in us, an image of a world and of ourselves that is perfect, but our actions and our lives clash with these expectations and hopes. When we realize the painful brokenness of relationships, a world of violence and deceit, a society of abuse, and contrast it with our desire for justice, peace, beauty, truth, holiness, and wholeness, we become aware of this chasm.

Christianity does not accept this abyss but explains it by pointing to the disobedience of Adam and Eve. This does not mean that the primal act of disobedience must have happened in a paradisiacal garden or was about eating from a tree: the story of the Fall explains with a myth what is the theological core of the story, namely, that humans acted against God. The question of when that happened is certainly interesting but does not really help. After all, the apocryphal book of 2 Enoch muses that the Fall happened only five and a half hours after Adam and Eve began living in paradise together.[2] That seems to me a very realistic assessment of human strength and weakness and a wonderful reminder of how long we can do without God: we can only hold out for a few hours without Christ's grace.

The disrupted relationship with God is the effect of the Fall, which was a willful act of disobedience toward God. Catholic dogma also states that the lifting of original sin that happens in baptism does not wipe out its worldly effects—our experience of unfulfilled desire and our inability to "walk a straight line" without grace. Thus, original sin remains a true mystery that cannot be proven, much like the Trinity or the virgin birth. Yet we can see, as I said in the previous chapter, that our grim and self-absorbed world makes sense if we believe in original sin.

True Freedom

When I read the biblical text of Genesis, chapters two and three, with my university students, I ask them why God forbade Adam and Eve from eating from one tree only. "Perhaps he wanted to test them" or "Because he knew they would fail" are among the most common answers. I think Aquinas gave a better explanation—as usual. He said that man and woman could eat whatever they wanted and do whatever they wanted since the moral law was their true nature. Thus following the moral law did not really entice a free decision—just as a well-tempered person is not acting heroically if he is not bursting into temper tantrums, because it is not in his nature. For a number of scholastic authors, God wanted humans to do one thing only because he desired it. By propagating this specific law, "You are free to eat from any of the trees of the garden except the tree of knowledge of good and evil. From that tree you shall not eat; when you eat from it you shall die" (Gn 2:16–17), he challenged the freedom of Adam and Eve.

Now they had to make a free decision. It would be wrong to state that they *had* to act against God's will in order to exercise their freedom or that in the act of disobedience lay their true emancipation from God. After all, it is through God's law that the human person realizes his vocation. By violating the law, the human person throws himself back into the abyss of egocentrism, while acting according to God's will is "an act of perfect freedom."[3] That is why Catholics venerate Mary's decision to become the handmaid of the Lord in the Incarnation as an act of perfect freedom. The question, "Could she have said no?" is wrongheaded, since she was protected from the stain of original sin and from all egocentrism. Thus she was free to say yes and had the most perfect freedom of all created beings.

Original sin is therefore not about personal guilt—indeed, the baby to be baptized is incapable of such. It is, however, the truth about human society. We are not born into the "people of God"—we have to join the Church. We step into Christian life, and without doing so we lack something—we lack the quality of being adopted children of God.

Thus, the doctrine reminds us that we as humans are all connected in a web of guilt, of collective sin and destruction, from which we have to free ourselves. Baptism offers the grace to do so, but it does not take the wound off our soul, as Benedict Groeschel used to say; it merely makes sure that the wound scars over, but it does not make it disappear.[4]

Repentance Is No Hangover

God not only punishes wrongdoing but also offers salvation and forgiveness to those who repent and are reborn in him. We talk today far too little about the positive aspects of penance. Instead, some make fun of the arguably painful penance rituals of the Middle Ages or of a Catholic "guilt complex." Others, who want to be supermodern, even suggest that repentance is unnecessary; we just have to make things better next time.

Repentance, however, is not the fear of possible punishment or the wish to undo the past (which would be impossible). If that is what repentance means to Christians, then it would indeed be cowardice on steroids or simply the inability to take responsibility for our actions.[5] Repentance also is not a moral "hangover," felt after the delightful consequences of a bad action wane. If the fear or hangover theory were correct, then repentance would be meaningless, or perhaps even harmful.

The Christian tradition conceived repentance as a form of self-healing of the soul, a way to regain its lost powers. "It is something . . . more: it is the natural function with which God endowed the soul, in order that the soul might return to him whenever it strayed from him."[6] I think Max Scheler had a really important insight here. He analyzed in depth why people have such wrongheaded understandings of repentance, and he realized that these misconceptions stemmed from false ideas about the *structure* of their spiritual life.

By remembering the past, we redeem it and free the present from its ballast. It is as if we took out of a river the bulky items that destroy a dam and turn it into a dangerous stream. If we remember our bad deeds, we reduce the deadly pressure and tame the past, which would otherwise determine our future by ripping apart the riverbed of our soul. As Scheler notes, "Repentance kills the life-nerve of guilt's action and continuance. It drives motive and deed—the deed with its root—out of the living center of the self, and thereby enables life to begin."[7] Remembering, of course, does not mean just making a mental image of the past or an image of the past action we repent. By remembering, we deliberately and intentionally repossess something of the past in us and relive it. That allows us to judge it and reject it in the act of repentance. This action requires the willingness to repent.

Redemption from Guilt

The hardest part of repentance seems to be not so much the confessional element but rather self-surrender to the divine law. In repenting, we acknowledge that we could have acted differently, and thus remember dynamically and intentionally, and we perceive a higher dimension of moral responsibility.

Repentance enables us to disown the powers of guilt. In the act of repentance, we intentionally move our mind toward our guilt and thus cease its controlling power. Therefore, it is a complete misunderstanding to think of Catholicism as a guilt-ridden religion. Instead, it attempts to free men and women from the power of guilt as it frees them from the bonds of the sinful life, through repentance. It should become clear how such an intentional remembering is a transformative and rejuvenating power.

Only through repentance for our sins do we realize that life does not have to follow the necessary and determined paths of nature—that there exists a way to life and a lifting of guilt. This process begins by accusing oneself of the bad actions one has done, as well as the good actions one has not done—a truth Pope Francis often reminds us about and a practice he learned from the writings of St. Ignatius of Loyola.[8]

The God that Ignatius envisions is the God of love and mercy and forgiveness, but he is also the God who despises the cheap excuses humans make for their pleasure-seeking actions. A nice god might pardon us without care for our repentance, but so would a terrible parent who is not interested in us becoming mature and responsible persons. The God of Christians, however, is a "jealous" God (Ex 20:4–5), meaning that he desires to transform us fully and not just superficially. The reality of original sin and the possibility of forgiveness and repentance in the Christian tradition demonstrate the far superior vision of a God who really cares for our fulfillment in all eternity.

While a worldly judge is interested in a confession and a superficial show of regret, God asks contrition of us, because it is the rejuvenating well of transformation. When we respond with the disposition of contrition, we reject our sins and our allegiance to them. It is an intentional act that includes self-surrender to a merciful God. This is different from a bad conscience: When we have a bad conscience, we know that there is something wrong with us, but we do not make it the center of our attention and articulate a clear accusation as to what we have done wrong. Thus, this knowledge of our moral state remains sterile and does not contribute to our moral progress. The disposition of contrition, however, always contains a relational aspect: it desires to reestablish the community with God that has been weakened or destroyed, and also entails the renunciation of future sins.[9]

Confession of our sins is essentially related to God's grace and the ability we have, through him, to be reborn. The New Testament shows that God is not someone who wants to give us a nice hug but one who expects us to become holy (and thus different from this world), who expects us to accuse ourselves of our sins and root out the evil in our hearts. This is clear from the encounter of Jesus with Nicodemus (Jn 3:1–7):

> Now there was a Pharisee named Nicodemus, a ruler of the Jews. He came to Jesus at night and said to him, "Rabbi, we know that you are a teacher who has come from God, for no one can do these signs that you are doing unless God is with him." Jesus answered and said to him, "Amen, amen, I say to you, no one can see the kingdom of God without being born from above." Nicodemus said to him, "How can a person once grown old be

born again? Surely he cannot reenter his mother's womb and be born again, can he?" Jesus answered, "Amen, amen, I say to you, no one can enter the kingdom of God without being born of water and Spirit. What is born of flesh is flesh and what is born of spirit is spirit. Do not be amazed that I told you, 'You must be born from above.'"

Being born from above is a gift of grace that requires the self-surrender of one's flesh, blood, and mind. We can learn from the saints how to repent. Then we understand why they thought of themselves as the greatest sinners—not because they suffered from hysteria but because they had learned to love and surrender. Just as only a lot of light can shine into the darkest corners, a person who loves God can see her own insufficiencies better than a person who still awaits such transformation.

THE ADVENTUROUS GOD

We had a nice vacation" is a description I would expect to hear from an elderly couple returning from a week-long trip to the Wisconsin Dells, where they soaked in hot tubs and enjoyed all-you-can-eat buffets. I would never expect Theodore Roosevelt, returning from his 1914 expedition to South America, to refer to his trip as "nice." In fact, Roosevelt, known to be a force of nature himself, abhorred an uneventful life as one not worth living. Nice is the opposite of eventful and adventurous; moreover, *weak*, *safe*, and *comfortable* can be synonyms for *nice*, while *strong*, *powerful*, and *adventurous* seem to be its antonyms.

If God Isn't Nice

Hopefully by now I have convinced you that God is not nice—nor should we *want* God to be nice. Now, let's explore other qualities of God, and explanations of God, that theologians have created that are similar to niceness.

Suppose for a moment that God is weak. What would this mean? Weak is the opposite of strong and is incompatible with omnipotence. A weak god could not have created the universe. Some might ask, Was it even God who created the world? Could it not be that the universe is eternal, just like God?

If that were the case, then God is not all-powerful because something exists that he cannot change—namely, the universe and, with it, space and time. If the universe is eternal, God might have enough power to create some things, but would he be a God worthy of reverence and prayer? If he could merely persuade stardust to take certain forms, he would not be the reason of all existence but just a part of it.

There are theologians who propose just such a concept of God—they are called "process theologians." For them, God is part of the world process just as we are, albeit more powerful. Nevertheless, this process god is really quite weak. He is limited in many ways, especially in his relationships. Since he is not the source of all being, he could never be the force that keeps the universe and us in existence.

While traditional theology maintains that the all-powerful God created the universe and keeps it every moment in existence and is as close to us as to every atom in creation, a process god would have a different relationship to us. We would be part of something that is beyond him, namely the material world, and thus not more than Pinocchios, string puppets set together by a higher intelligence. Such a god would obviously not be able to give eternal life because he has no control over space and time; he would not be able to save us from sin and evil because he is not God.

Such a god reminds me of the depiction of God in the Star Trek movie *The Final Frontier*. Spock's half-brother Sybok leads the starship *Enterprise* to a planet beyond the border of the universe, where supposedly God awaits them. Indeed, the crew meets a spiritual being that is extremely powerful. It desires to board the starship so that its "glory" can be brought to the universe. Captain Kirk asks it the crucial question: "Why does God need a starship?" The god the *Enterprise* crew encounters is a powerful being—an alien but not God. This being is terrifying but does not leave Kirk in awe and wonder about its beauty and goodness; instead, it makes him frown. Its appearance makes him suspicious.

When one stands in front of God, one knows. This is a simple truth all mystics of all religions agree on. A weak god would be better dead and buried than presented in a classroom of religious education. Such a god would not be worth worshiping or worth even a ticket on a starship—not only because he would not be the source of all that is but also because he could not be the God who offers help, or, as Christians call it, salvation. When Christians express their belief in Jesus Christ as their Savior, they are expressing their conviction that God the Father, who has created everything that is, has opened the path to eternal communion with him—a path that was closed before. After all, we confess, "and his kingdom will have no end"!

Re-Enchanting the World

Perhaps nobody has expressed the importance of adventure better than G. K. Chesterton. His works are overflowing with descriptions of how a nice and weak god would be uneventful and predictable, and of how our soul yearns for an adventure with God.[1] A weak god would not want us to radically change but would be content with a spiritual face-lift. The God of Jesus Christ, however, is the one who takes us, like the Lord himself, out on a lake awaiting a storm (Mk 4:35).

A process god could be a source of comfort, keeping our feet warm, our hands clean, and our brains occupied with thoughts about morality—perhaps. Yet one would do better to live by a rule of philosophical principles such as Immanuel Kant's "Act according to the maxim that you would wish all other rational people to follow, as if it were a universal law," or the Golden Rule, than to rely upon a kind process grandpa-god in heaven.

God is full of surprises, and so is life. Chesterton once remarked that the real adventure in life is not found when we leave our homes for a new frontier, be it in the wilderness, research, or love. Rather, adventure is to be found in the midst of where each individual lives, in our own homes.[2] Could you imagine climbing down your chimney and traveling through your living room as if it were the Amazon? Could you encounter your own children as if you had just found a new animal species? Do a little experiment! Look around and identify the first table you see. Now close your eyes, imagine it, and give it a different name; for example, call it *tish*. Keep the image in your mind, your eyes closed, and repeat the table's new name, *tish*, slowly about ten times. When you open your eyes and see the *tish*, it will look strange to you, and you will see it in a new and different light, as if you had discovered it.[3] This is the sort of thing Chesterton had in mind with his program of "re-enchanting" our world. It does not mean inventing imaginary friends or sprites but rather rediscovering the awe-inspiring joy we experienced when we first encountered things—the experience of children.

A God of Surprises

How does the foregoing relate to God? God is a force that surprises and enchants, a being that is life in its fullness. God is adventure.

Christians believe that the human experience with God resulted in holy books. Although so many of our contemporaries are bored with the Church and God, you will not find a single line in the Bible that says life with God is dull. Why? Because the writers of these texts knew, guided by the Holy Spirit, that a life with God is an adventurous journey.

Take, for example, the book of Genesis: It recounts how the world and humans were created, leaving aside the question of whether this happened in six days or billions of years ago. Instead, it invites us to focus on the story *itself*. God endows his first creature, Adam, with the right to name everything in creation. If I name something, I have power over it and know its meaning and nature, the ancient Hebrews believed. Thus, by naming the things of the world, Adam participates in the kingship of God over all that is. Normally only God would give things and beings their names, but he delegates this task to Adam. Like a child who is given all the toys imaginable, Adam is allowed to give all things names. It is Adam's joy of insight, surprise, and awe that we usually fail to see in this episode.

Adam is depicted as not just the first human being but also the guardian of the world, who received great honor and responsibility from God. In the next chapter of Genesis, this partaking in divine kingship is suddenly abused. Both Adam and his wife, Eve, become weak in the moment of temptation. Both rationalize choosing evil. Suddenly, the fruit of the forbidden tree looks good, wholesome, and attractive. We know what happens next—both are expelled from paradise and are punished by the divine lawgiver.

God allowed the Fall to happen because he gave both persons full freedom to make a decision against his will. By endowing Adam and Eve with free will, God decided that he did not want to have a kindergarten universe surrounded by high walls to prevent people from falling over the edge. In such a world we could not get hurt, nor could we hurt others. Every hurtful word would be turned into praise, and every fist transformed into a sign of peace. It would be a world in which moral zombies could live but not humans. It would be a world without adventure—a bloodless, boring universe.

God wants the adventure of free will, the Bible tells us, because true freedom consists in fulfillment: only if we fill our heart with the infinite will we find rest, as St. Augustine said, and satisfaction. Freedom in the traditional and Christian understanding is the adventure of doing the right thing, whereby grace does not enslave us but liberates us to be truly free.

This is important to emphasize, because the media and politics tell us that freedom is always and only "freedom of choice." If there are not at least two options, it is not real freedom, we are told. In the Christian worldview (and in the tradition of philosophy from Cicero to Aquinas), *freedom is always freedom to do good*: if my life is shaped by sins, I am not free. Instead, I am like an addict, chained to my habits. Is a drug addict facing a table loaded with forbidden narcotics free because he can theoretically walk away or because he can choose only to take a minimal amount of his favorite drug? I do not think so. I rather believe that such a person's ability to be free and fulfill the plan God placed in his heart is severely diminished! It is God's love—we call it grace—that sets us free and empowers us to break the chains of our addictions and sins. It is grace if we think in the morning as we wake up, "Will I be able to live up to God's expectations today?" and it is grace if I am able to persevere in temptation.

Human beings are God's greatest adventure. Of course, God is omniscient regarding all our actions and thoughts, but he leaves us our freedom and seems to choose to be surprised. I cannot help but compare this to my own parenting. When my younger children prepare a surprise present for my birthday, I usually find traces in the kitchen and the living room: crayons, pieces of paper, glue sticks, and first drafts with "Happy Birthday" on them. Nevertheless, I choose to be surprised when they hand me their work of art. I think that with an omniscient God, it must be somehow like this.

A nice, predictable process god would not care for adventure. Such a god would prefer the material comfort of a sofa over the excitement of having children, the security of savings over the adventure of making ends meet, and the sobriety of a single glass of port over drunkenness with love and ecstasy. Such a god is hardly compatible with the accounts of the Bible.

The Adventures of Noah, Abraham, and Moses

Consider the stories of some of the great adventurers of the Old Testament as clear evidence that the God of the Bible dislikes a convenient lifestyle and armchair theologians. Noah, the book of Genesis narrates, was a just man in a world of humans who had forgotten their duties toward one another, nature, and God. As a punishment, God sends a flood to wipe out the sinners. He does not choose to comfortably translocate Noah and his family to a safe place but rather puts the survival of humankind and the animal kingdom in Noah's hands. Noah is charged with building the ark and saving all species of animals. By building the ship, Noah offends everybody around him. Why? Because he claims God has spoken to him and uttered a judgment against them. Noah excludes them and reminds them of their wrongdoing. Nobody wants to look in the mirror and be reminded of his sins! Yet God expects Noah to persevere in being the outsider. God's history with Noah is not easy, but it is not unbearable; and because he perseveres, a new covenant is set in the sky, a rainbow that represents God's promise never to destroy the earth again. God did, of course, foreknow all of what would happen, but as Rudolph Otto said, in line with our discussion in a previous chapter, the ancient writers used the image of God changing his mind to express the terrifying awe we feel when we face God's plans.

God is good at surprises, but he is not like a wavering friend who first wants to come over for dinner and then not, because he does not change his eternal will. It only appears to us as if he sometimes has done so. This must be of some significance. It seems to me, however, that the old claim that the story of the flood intends to illustrate that God's power is limitless and that he is the ultimate sovereign is a bit too flat. It leaves out the magic of the story.

The God of the Bible is a God who wants us to be adventurous people. He wants us to get up, find him, listen to him, and set sail. Another story might be even better to exemplify this, namely, the one about Abraham's vocation. God calls Abraham to leave everything behind—his family, his property, his homeland and native language—and go to a land God will show him. It is safe to say that Abraham's closest relatives thought he was crazy. Who would leave everything behind to follow a God without a name on a journey with an unknown destiny?

Moses's story is similarly a challenge of trust: Will Moses trust in the adventure God has prepared for him? We must not forget who this Moses is—a murderer. In sheer rage, he had killed an Egyptian guard, and God still maintains his plan that Moses is the one to free his people from slavery in Egypt, just as he chooses another murderer (by proxy) about 1,400 years later to spread the Gospel, St. Paul.

We can also understand the escape from Egypt and the so-called exodus, the forty years wandering in the desert, in the light of adventure. The Israelites are fed daily by bread from heaven, manna, and by meat from heaven in the form of quails. The hungry refugees are told directly by God that they cannot store any of the sweet, waferlike bread; instead, they must await it every day. They have to trust God every day to be fed. For most people living in the Western world, having access to clean water and plenty of food is taken for granted. The Israelites, who previously had been held as slaves in Egypt, probably did not have to go to bed hungry but received food from their masters.

Now, however, in the life-threatening conditions of the desert, they are asked to trust, just as Abraham trusted an unknown God. Many had no doubt forgotten the tales of their fathers about Abraham, Isaac, and Jacob, and many had certainly ceased to pray to a God who left them in the misery of slavery. Now they have to trust this God every day, although they do not know him. They have to trust so much that it hurts. Not so much as a crumb of bread can they keep from the manna for themselves. Every piece of manna deteriorates by the next day.

Trusting somebody you do not know is a risky business. Trusting a God you do not know comes close to insanity—at least in the eyes of the world. Yet Moses admonishes his people to do just that, to cast off their fear and engage in the adventure that God had prepared for them.

The Greatest Adventure of All

Now, there is one adventure that surpasses all. Christians believe that the eternal God, who existed before all time, decided to become human in Jesus Christ. Two thousand years ago, this idea seemed perhaps even more scandalous than today.

Many ancient religions venerated gods that were believed to have taken on human form, but the Incarnation of Jesus, as Christians understood it, was different. Jesus did not cloak himself in human flesh in order to impregnate women as Jupiter did, nor did he intervene in battles with divine powers as in Troy. Instead, the God of Jesus Christ decided to receive his humanity from a teenage virgin named Mary and to be born as every other child, passing through the birth canal and exploring the world through the eyes of a creaturely body. No other religion had conceived of such a God, who submits completely to the conditions of human life.

The New Testament does not tell us much about the early life of Jesus, but it mentions that he left his parents and remained in the Temple arguing with the best theologians of the time. The only story about Jesus' childhood, apart from the account of his nativity, is a story about the adventure of a young boy who discovers that he is different from others. Without the protection of his family against robbers or cutthroats, he wanders around the Temple!

We do not know Jesus' whereabouts for the next twenty years. After the incident in the Temple, the New Testament says only that he "obeyed his parents and grew wiser." This sounds like a pretty boring life—staying home with Mom and Dad, doing their will. If we think that, we have not comprehended the story.

We have to read it from Jesus' perspective: the Son of God decides to live for the next twenty years in obedience to two earthly creatures, who are wise and good but are still *his* creatures. He desires to learn their ways and the ways of humans around them. God in Jesus submits to the restrictions of earthly life. If we put it that way, it sounds like an awful sacrifice, as if we asked a pop star to live for two decades in a one-bedroom apartment with our grandmother. But the point is that God undergoes the experience of human life from the perspective of a creature. The limitless divine being limits itself to a creaturely life.

The human nature of Jesus even experienced pain. The first theologians of Christianity, the Church Fathers, mostly bishops of the first few centuries, stated boldly that "one of the Holy Trinity [Father, Son, and Spirit]" has suffered. The pain that Jesus in his human nature feels is also felt by the second person of the Trinity.

For the Greek philosophers of antiquity, the idea of a suffering God would have been scandalous. As an all-perfect being, God cannot suffer because pain is the absence of happiness; since God is perfectly happy, he cannot suffer. Only if one assumes that God temporarily suspends some of his characteristics and limits himself to the earthly body of Jesus can one fathom a suffering God.

Christians believe that the Incarnation happened only once— *could* happen only once—because, through it, the role of the Trinity was revealed to all human beings. In Jesus, God has spoken his last word.

What most do not reflect upon, however, is that this experience of suffering was something entirely new for God—in a sense, an adventure. No, I do not propose that God changes or that God needs us or human history to become his true "self," as the German philosopher Hegel (and unfortunately quite a few theologians) thought, but that the pain the Son of God felt through the human nature of Jesus was something special. I am not just talking of the Passion and Crucifixion but the pain Jesus experienced throughout the thirty-three years of his earthly existence.

It began with the pain of passing through the birth canal, the pain of circumcision, the pain of moving to Egypt and back, the pain of losing his father Joseph, the pain of losing friends to death. Moreover, the other limitations of an earthly life were new to God. Of course, he knew that creatures had to be fed, but now he experienced hunger and thirst and—as a result of the Fall of Adam and Eve—the need to work for one's own sustenance. Exegetes agree that Jesus learned the craft of carpentry. For decades he worked in the heat of the Palestinian sun to earn his wages, probably endured sickness at times and enjoyed health at others, and stayed with his family. It amazes me that even most books about the historical Jesus hardly ever mention the last point.

From the New Testament we know of the brothers of Jesus, with whom he lived for quite some time. An old tradition sees the brothers as Joseph's sons from a previous marriage and thus as stepbrothers of Jesus. He probably went to his siblings' weddings, learned to dance, and celebrated the births of their children but also grieved for their deaths. This side of his life was also part of God's adventure in the Incarnation—to experience the joys of being human. Growing up in a loving, holy family seems to have been a crucial part of Jesus' life.

The importance of Jesus' "hidden years," as the time is called about which we have no information, roughly from his twelfth to his thirtieth year of life, came to me when I read J. R. R. Tolkien's The Lord of the Rings. Frodo, who is entrusted with the greatest mission Middle-earth has ever seen—to destroy the ring of power—is the "most unlikely" creature to successfully complete this task.[4] He is young, inexperienced in adventure, not overly strong or muscular—but he has one characteristic that helps him to endure even the greatest challenges: he is virtuous. He grew up in a family that loved him, and in this family he learned to do good and to avoid evil. He made this a habit for himself. Good habits easily become virtues, because they deeply engrain themselves in our soul. Only because Frodo learned such virtues was he able to persevere in situations where more likely superheroes—like the clever elves or the strong dwarfs—would have failed. The earthly Jesus also had to learn the virtues of justice, temperance, prudence, and fortitude by living an ordinary life. He needed those years of preparation so that his final mission on Mount Calvary could be successful.

If It Is Good Enough for Jesus . . .

The Incarnation makes clear, in my view, that God wanted not only to expiate our sins and to teach us about himself but also to know what it feels like to be human. How was it for God to obey the earthly couple of Mary and Joseph, to experience pain and joy, and also to follow the Bible and obey the divine commandments? He learned firsthand how it was to live according to God's will. Thus, when Jesus suggested that following the commandments was life-giving, that pain can redeem us and help us become more mature persons, he was speaking from his own experience.

Looking through Jesus' eyes, God gains a new perspective about the intensity of love, suffering, and pain and thus sanctifies every human body. If the frail body that so easily withers away after a vigorous youth is good enough for God, then it is good enough for me. There is no greater act of solidarity that he could have made with us than to walk in our shoes, not just for a day but for thirty-three years. This is a God of adventure.

EPILOGUE

While I am proposing that we rediscover the adventure of faith, I do not want to eclipse the reality that starting such a new journey can be frightening. It was for me, too, because I did not know what would await me around the next corner on my path. After all, I left my Bavarian home to start a family in the United States, began to teach and write in a foreign language, and worked in a different university system. Yet knowing that I was not alone out at sea but rather have a sail, soulmate, and steady compass in Christ, has helped me maneuver the ship of my life.

Sometimes the uncertainty of the future scares us into desiring a straight path for life and a detailed road map of what we want to achieve and when. Most of the time, though, such plans are illusions, and sometimes we create similar illusions about God because we are afraid to encounter the real thing. But if I live in a religious la-la land because I fear changing my life for the one worth living for, I will ultimately fail and die a spiritual death. Conversely, if I expose myself to the object of my fear, I can turn that fear into hope. By learning to trust Jesus on the way, step by step, the fear of the unknown becomes the hope for love and fulfillment.[1]

This change is not easy, and as Dietrich von Hildebrand said, such an adventure to transformation requires complete surrender.

Surrender does not happen once and for all; such conversion and submission to God in will and intellect are asked of us every day, every hour, and we have to be honest enough to realize that we will only make progress with the help of grace.

That is why the adventure with God, the real God, leads to the sacraments. It is there where we can meet him more intimately than anywhere else and where our mind and heart have to be most attentive to perceive him. There cannot be an adventure of faith without the encouragement of the confessional, the road map of holy scripture, the food of the Holy Eucharist, and the fellowship of the Holy Spirit in our parishes.

It is this fellowship that brings together all the different aspects this book has tried to lay out. While we form our own imagination, and experience in our own bodies the terrifying, consoling, and enchanting mystery of God, we nevertheless are not alone on our journey. There are people all around us, many of whom we are connected to through bonds of family, love, and friendship and many more with whom we share a Church. We should remember that the way we live our faith permeates our being and is perceivable to others. I do not think we should disguise our real feelings and only smile in church and talk constantly about Jesus' love, because that would either be hypocritical or overwhelming.

So how do we find the right way to integrate faith into our lives? I think that is asking the wrong question. Instead, we should seek to integrate our lives into the faith. After all, Jesus does not become a part of us, but we become a part of his mystical body, the Church. We have to be integrated. With that in mind, we can see more clearly the priorities we have to pursue. In a world that is becoming increasingly hostile to the Christian faith, fellowship is more and more important—not just as a means of dispensing the sacraments, but as communities where transformation can be perceived. Many of us find it difficult to carve out extra time for meetings with other families because our kids or aging parents need attention, but our witness of perseverance in the pews every Sunday and in the confessional is equally important. Even if you do not participate in a parish committee or other such work, do not underestimate your quiet witness of prayer.

Writing this epilogue, I look at my statue of St. Joseph in my garden; he looks right into our family room, holding the Christ child in his arms. I like the fact that he "looks out for us"—quite literally. This view brings back a memory: A few years ago, I organized a lecture series for my hometown in Germany, and I was lucky enough to book a wonderful speaker to give a talk entitled "Women in the Church." After the talk, a young man and father asked the question, "After such a beautiful description of women's vocations in the Church, how can I as a man live my faith better?" The female speaker was for a moment puzzled, but as she contemplated her answer, she noticed the ten-foot-tall baroque painting of St. Joseph on the wall behind the man. She said, "Turn around: there is your answer." That stuck with me.

St. Joseph, often depicted as cooking food for the Christ child, working with the young Jesus in his shop, or holding a lily to symbolize both his purity and the fragrance of his grace-filled persona, never speaks in the New Testament. Instead, he is always acting. He is always there. When the shepherds arrive, they find "Mary and Joseph, and the infant" (Lk 2:16); only at the arrival of the Magi is he missing from the scene (Mt 2:11). Then, in the Gospel of Matthew, where God speaks to Joseph about the danger of Herod killing all infants born in Bethlehem, what we might miss is that he got up immediately, not the next day, and still by night departed in order to save his family (Mt 2:14).

Joseph is never absent, and he never wavers in his faith. That is why he has become the role model of fortitude. He holds on to what he knows is good, to what he knows is from God, however hard the road ahead of him might look. That, however, does not mean that he fully understands what is happening. When Simeon holds the baby Jesus in his arms and praises God that he has finally "seen salvation," Joseph is, like Mary, amazed (Lk 2:33). Like Mary, he does not understand what the twelve-year-old Jesus tells them after they find him in the Temple (Lk 2:48–50); yet Jesus returns with them to Nazareth and is obedient to them while growing in wisdom and favor before God (Lk 2:52). The fact that Jesus returned with his family gives us a clue about the importance of family and fellowship: Jesus is supposed to grow up and experience a family life in faith and devotion to God; it prepares him for his mission.

While there can never be enough said about Jesus and Mary, I would like to point at the end of this book to this forgotten hero of faith, Joseph. God was Joseph's real adventure: he decided to put aside his own wishes and desires for the one true God, the only one worth living for. He does not look at all like a hero at first sight; he is always simply, quietly, and prayerfully following the path God lays out in front of him. When disaster strikes, he does give in to rage, but he holds on to his righteousness. When his betrothed is suddenly found pregnant, he is surprised, probably even shocked. Yet instead of delivering her to public shame and humiliation, he wants to do the right thing and "divorce her quietly" (Mt 1:19). Again, Joseph's faith is not loud, not overbearing, but quiet. He is a man of integrity, a man who holds on to the good with a strong grip—the definition of fortitude! Only when the angel tells him in a dream to not be afraid of taking Mary as his wife does he change his mind and accept the adventure God puts before him: "When Joseph awoke, he did as the angel of the Lord had commanded him and took his wife into his home" (Mt 1:24).

Perhaps that is why Joseph is the patron saint of the Church. He prepared a home for the Incarnate Word; it dwelled in his house.

Opening the door is always dangerous, because one never knows who will come in. But only if we open the door of our soul do we have a chance of Jesus dwelling in us.

ACKNOWLEDGMENTS

The (now defunct) Earhart Foundation graciously supported me in writing a book on the history of sentimentalism and theology. When I began writing, I realized that it had real practical relevance for catechesis and the life of every Catholic. I therefore completely reworked it to make it more accessible.

Without the support of my dear friends Francesca Murphy (Notre Dame), D. Stephen Long (Southern Methodist University), and Matthew Levering (Mundelein Seminary), I would have never dared to leave my usual terrain of history for a more systematic approach to theology. I also thank my colleague and friend Mickey Mattox, who first introduced me to the idea that God was not nice. Finally, I thank Scott Hahn (Franciscan University of Steubenville) for his most gracious foreword.

I dedicate this book in gratitude to my teachers in theology, Gerhard Cardinal Müller and the late Frs. Joseph Waas, Karl Haller, and P. Giovanni Sala, S.J. They always reminded me of the wise whom the prophet Daniel spoke about: "Those with insight shall shine brightly like the splendor of the firmament" (Dn 12:3).

NOTES

Foreword

1. H. Richard Niebuhr, *The Kingdom of God in America* (1937; Middletown, CT: Wesleyan, 1988), 193.

1. The God of Creation

1. Erich Fromm, *To Have or to Be?* (New York: Harper and Row, 1976). Many new editions are also available.

2. Hans-Eduard Hengstenberg uses the word *sachlich*, which in this context means not simply objective.

3. There are, of course, many good works that introduce the reader to the philosophy of Thomas Aquinas. My favorites are Antoine Sertillanges, *Foundations of Thomistic Philosophy* (Springfield, IL: Templegate, 1956) and Jacques Maritain, *An Introduction to Philosophy* (many editions).

4. Cf. Hans-Eduard Hengstenberg, *Philosophische Anthropologie* (Stuttgart: Kohlhammer, 1957). Helmuth Plessner, *Die Stufen des Organischen und der Mensch* (1928; Berlin: DeGruyter, 2000); for an English exposition of Plessner, see Wolfhart Pannenberg, *Anthropology in Theological Perspective* (1985; Edinburgh: T and T Clark, 1999), especially 37–41.

5. Hans-Eduard Hengstenberg, *Christliche Grundhaltungen* (Kevalaer: Butzon und Bercker, 1938), 34.

6. Kenda Creasy Dean, *Almost Christian: What the Faith of Our Teenagers Is Telling the American Church* (New York: Oxford University Press, 2010).

7. Every parent should read Anthony Esolen, *Ten Ways to Destroy the Imagination of Your Child*, 2nd ed. (Wilmington, DE: Intercollegiate Studies Institute, 2013).

8. I rely here on the insights of Gabriel Marcel, *The Mystery of Being*, 2 vols. (1949–1950; South Bend, IN: St. Augustine's Press, 2001).

9. James V. Schall, *The Order of Things* (San Francisco: Ignatius Press, 2007).

10. Theologians have, like bishops, neglected the role of children, although they could learn much from them. See Gustav Siewerth, *Metaphysik der Kindheit* (Einsiedeln: Johannes Verlag, 1965).

11. The best reading about this is, I believe, still Aristotle's *Metaphysics*, book 4.

12. On theories of truth, a good introduction is found in J. P. Moreland and William L. Craig, *Philosophical Foundations of a Christian Worldview* (Downers Grove, IL: InterVarsity Press, 2003), 130–154; for a witty dialogue demonstrating the falsehood of relativism, see Peter Kreeft, *A Refutation of Moral Relativism: Interviews with an Absolutist* (San Francisco, CA: Ignatius Press, 1999).

13. Max Picard, *The Flight from God*, trans. Marianne Kuschnitsky and J. M. Cameron (1935; South Bend, IN: St. Augustine's Press, 2015).

14. Hengstenberg, *Christliche Grundhaltungen*, 130–131.

15. Josef Pieper, *The Four Cardinal Virtues: Prudence, Justice, Fortitude, Temperance* (1954; Notre Dame, IN: University of Notre Dame Press, 1966); see the chapter on fortitude.

16. Ibid., 137.

17. Hans-Eduard Hengstenberg, *Einsamkeit und Tod* (Regensburg: Pustet, 1938).

2. The God of No Use

1. Keiji Nishitani, *Religion and Nothingness* trans. Jan Van Bragt (Berkeley: University of California Press, 1983), 1–45.

2. Robert Spaemann, *Das unsterbliche Gerücht: Die Frage nach Gott und die Täuschung der Moderne* (Stuttgart: Klett Cotta, 2007), 92–120.

3. Ibid., 106.

4. Nishitani, *Religion*, 3.

5. Bernhard Rosenmöller, *Religionsphilosophie*, 2nd ed. (Münster: Aschendorff, 1939), 68–69.

6. John S. Dunne, *The City of the Gods: A Study in Myth and Mortality* (Notre Dame, IN: University of Notre Dame Press, 1978).

7. Thomas V. Morris, *Making Sense of It All: Pascal and the Meaning of Life* (Grand Rapids, MI: Eerdmans, 1992), 35–36.

8. Max Scheler, *Vom Ewigen im Menschen* (Leipzig: Verlag der neue Geist, 1921), 647f.; Johannes Hessen, *Die Werte des Heiligen* (Regensburg: Pustet, 1938).

9. Scheler, *Vom Ewigen*, 658f.

10. Ibid., 666.

11. Spaemann, *Das unsterbliche Gerücht*, 157.

12. But let's look at the statement "Rape is always immoral," for example. I hope every reader agrees with this statement and would agree that its validity is independent of culture and context. If so, then you have agreed to the existence of objective moral norms and you might want to search for more than this one.

13. Spaemann, *Das unsterbliche Gerücht*, 164.

3. The God of Our Imagination

1. Joseph Ratzinger, *God and the World: A Conversation with Peter Seewald* (San Francisco: Ignatius Press, 2002), chapter titled "An Image of God."

2. Dietrich von Hildebrand, *Transformation in Christ: On the Christian Attitude* (1948; San Francisco: Ignatius Press, 2001), 5.

3. Adam Smith, *The Theory of Moral Sentiments* [1790]: *Glasgow Edition* (Indianapolis, IN: Liberty Fund, 1982), part VI, sect. II, chap. 3, 236.

4. Ryan Patrick Hanley, *Adam Smith and the Character of Virtue* (New York: Cambridge University Press, 2009), 198.

4. The God of Thunder

1. Alasdair MacIntyre, *After Virtue: A Study in Moral Theory* (Notre Dame, IN: University of Notre Dame Press, 1984).

5. The God of Terror

1. Origen, *On First Principles*, trans. G.W. Butterworth (London: SPCK, 1936), book 4, ch. 3, 288.

2. Augustine, *On Christian Doctrine*, III.10.14.

3. John Crowe Ransom, *God without Thunder* (London: G. Howe, 1931), 14.

4. My thoughts in this chapter are based on Rudolf Otto, *The Idea of the Holy* (1917; New York: Oxford University Press, 1958).

5. Thomas Aquinas, *Summa Theologiae*, I.12.12.

6. The God of Surrender

1. Ruby Blondell, *Helping Friends and Harming Enemies: A Study in Sophocles and Greek Ethics* (New York: Cambridge University Press, 1989).

2. Gerhard Lohfink, *No Irrelevant Jesus: On Jesus and the Church Today* (Collegeville, MN: Liturgical Press, 2014), chap. 5.

3. Cf. Josef Pieper, *About Love* (Chicago: Franciscan Herald Press, 1974), 20.

4. Gabriel Marcel, *Thou Shall Not Die*, ed. Anne Marcel (Notre Dame, IN: St. Augustine's Press, 2009).

5. My thoughts are based on Josef Pieper, *Faith, Hope, Love* (San Francisco: Ignatius Press, 1997), 139–282. I have used the German original, *Über die Liebe* (Munich: Kösel, 1972).

6. Aristotle, *Rhetoric*, book II, chap. 4, 1380b. http://data.perseus.org/citations/urn:cts:greekLit:tlg0086.tlg038.perseus-eng1:1380b.

7. *Weimarer Ausgabe* 36, 438, 21 (Homily on 1 Jn 4:16 of 16 June 1532), my translation.

8. Cf. Dietrich von Hildebrand, *The Nature of Love*, trans. John Crosby (Notre Dame, IN: St. Augustine's Press, 2009).

9. C. S. Lewis, *Mere Christianity: Comprising the Case for Christianity, Christian Behavior, and Beyond Personality* (New York: Touchstone, 1996), 105–106.

10. Lohfink, *No Irrelevant Jesus*, chap. 18.

7. The God of Intimacy

1. See Roger Scruton, *Sexual Desire: A Philosophical Investigation* (1986; New York: Continuum, 2006), chap. 3 ("Persons"), and his books *The Face of God* (New York: Continuum, 2012) and *The Soul of the World* (Princeton, NJ: Princeton University Press, 2014), chaps. 4 and 5.

2. Augustine, *Confessions*, III.6.11.

3. Fulton J. Sheen, *The Priest Is Not His Own* (1963; San Francisco: Ignatius Press, 2005), 11–14.

4. Franz Werfel, *Leben heisst sich mitteilen* (Frankfurt am Main: S. Fischer, 1992).

5. See chapter 9. In my remarks on why Jesus "had" to suffer, I rely on Harald Schöndorf, S.J., *Warum musste Jesus leiden? Eine neue Antwort auf eine alte Frage* (Munich: Pneuma, 2013).

6. Dorothy L. Sayers, *The Mind of the Maker* (1941; New York: Harper Collins, 1987), 187.

7. Ibid.

8. The God of Consolation

1. Karl Pfleger, *Nur das Mysterium tröstet* (Frankfurt: Knecht, 1957).

2. Blaise Pascal, *Pensées*, 139, quoted in Tom Morris, *Making Sense of It All: Pascal as a Guide to the Meaning of Life* (Grand Rapids, MI: Eerdmans, 1992), 32.

3. C. S. Lewis, *The Great Divorce: A Dream* (London: Geoffrey Bles, 1945), also available in many other editions.

4. Donald and Idella Gallagher, eds., *A Maritain Reader: Selected Writings* (Garden City, NY: Image Books, 1966), 111–112.

5. For an introduction to Comte's thought in this area, see Andrew Wernick, *Auguste Comte and the Religion of Humanity* (New York: Cambridge University Press, 2001).

6. Bertrand Russell, *Why I Am Not a Christian and Other Essays* (New York: Simon and Schuster, 1957), 107.

7. Schöndorf, *Warum musste Jesus leiden?*

8. Peter Wust, *Ungewissheit und Wagnis* (Salzburg: Pustet, 1937), and many new editions.

9. The God of Incarnation

1. Francis Maluf, "Sentimental Theology" (1947), http://catholicism.org/sentimental-theology.html.

2. C. S. Lewis, *The Problem of Pain* (1940; New York: Touchstone, 1996), 36.

3. Brian Kolodiejchuk, ed., *Mother Teresa: Come Be My Light: The Private Writings of the Saint of Calcutta* (New York: Doubleday, 2007); Thomas R. Nevin, *The Last Years of Saint Thérèse: Doubt and Darkness, 1895–1897* (New York: Oxford University Press, 2013).

4. Manfred Lütz, Lebenslust: *Wider die Dät-Sadisten, den Gesundheitswahn, und den Fitness-Kult* (Munich: Pattloch, 2007).

5. Taylor Caldwell, *The Listener* (New York: Doubleday, 1960), vii–viii.

6. Odo Marquard, *In Defense of the Accidental: Philosophical Studies*, trans. Robert M. Wallace (New York: Oxford University Press, 1991), 81.

7. G. K. Chesterton, *Orthodoxy* (1908; San Francisco: Ignatius Press, 1995), 145.

8. Brant Pitre, *Jesus and the Jewish Roots of the Eucharist: Unlocking the Secrets of the Last Supper* (New York: Doubleday, 2011).

9. Rodney Stark, *The Rise of Christianity: How the Obscure, Marginal Jesus Movement Became the Dominant Religious Force in the Western World in a Few Centuries* (New York: HarperOne, 1997), 177–178.

10. The God of Rebirth

1. Spaemann, *Das unsterbliche Gerücht*, 187.

2. Alan Jacobs, *Original Sin: A Cultural History* (New York: HarperOne, 2008), 43.

3. Spaemann, *Das unsterbliche Gerücht*, 203.

4. Benedict Groeschel, *Healing the Original Wound: Reflections on the Full Meaning of Salvation* (Ann Arbor, MI: Servant, 1993).

5. Scheler, *Vom Ewigen*, 10. An English translation of Scheler's essay "Repentance and Rebirth" is available in Max Scheler, *On the Eternal in Man* (New York: Transaction Publishers, 2010), 33–66.

6. Scheler, *Vom Ewigen*, 12.

7. Scheler, *On the Eternal*, 42.

8. Francis, *The Way of Humility: Corruption and Sin and On Self-Accusation* (San Francisco: Ignatius Press, 2014).

9. Hildebrand, *Transformation in Christ*, 31–52.

11. The Adventurous God

1. For a very short and brilliant introduction to Chesterton, I recommend Aidan Nichols, *G. K. Chesterton, Theologian* (Manchester, NH: Sophia Institute Press, 2009). An excellent book for the advanced theological reader is David W. Fagerberg, *The Size of Chesterton's Catholicism* (Notre Dame, IN: University of Notre Dame Press, 1998). In my view, the best biography is Joseph Pearce, *Wisdom and Innocence: A Life of G. K. Chesterton*, 2nd ed. (San Francisco: San Ignatius Press, 2015).

2. G. K. Chesterton, *The Collected Works, Vol. 1: Heretics, Orthodoxy, The Blatchford Controversies* (San Francisco: San Ignatius Press, 1986), 143.

3. For an introduction to such exercises, the following book is helpful: Roger-Pol Droit, *Astonish Yourself: 101 Experiments in the Philosophy of Everyday Life*, trans. Stephen Romer (New York: Penguin, 2003).

4. Readers who are unfamiliar with The Lord of the Rings saga and its theological background might want to consult Peter Kreeft, *The Philosophy of Tolkien* (San Francisco: Ignatius Press, 2005), or Ralph C. Wood, *The Gospel According to Tolkien: Visions of the Kingdom in Middle-Earth* (Louisville, KY: Westminster John Knox Press, 2003).

Epilogue

1. See, for example, Hans Urs von Balthasar, *The Christian and Anxiety*, trans. Adrian Walker (1952; San Francisco: Ignatius Press, 2000).

Ulrich L. Lehner is an internationally renowned professor of religious history and theology at Marquette University in Milwaukee, Wisconsin.

He is a native of Bavaria/Germany and has earned doctorates in history and theology. Among his numerous honors are grants and fellowships from the Princeton Institute for Advanced Study, the Notre Dame Institute for Advanced Study, and the Humboldt Foundation.

The author and editor of more than twenty books, Lehner received the John G. Shea Award for the best book on Catholic history in 2011 by the American Catholic Historical Association for *Enlightened Monks*. Since 2014, he is an elected member of the European Academy of Sciences and Arts.

Lehner lives in the Milwaukee area with his wife, Angela, and their five children.

AVE

AVE MARIA PRESS

Founded in 1865, Ave Maria Press,
a ministry of the Congregation of
Holy Cross, is a Catholic publishing
company that serves the spiritual and
formative needs of the Church and its
schools, institutions, and ministers;
Christian individuals and families; and
others seeking spiritual nourishment.

———◦◉◦———

For a complete listing of titles from

Ave Maria Press

Sorin Books

Forest of Peace

Christian Classics

visit avemariapress.com